Emma's Family

EDITED BY RONALD E. ROMIG

John Whitmer Books
2008

For Emma

Emma's Family
Edited by Ronald E. Romig
Published in the United States of America

John Whitmer Books
Independence, Missouri
www.JohnWhitmerBooks.com
ISBN 1-934901-24-5   ISBN13 978-1-934901-24-3
Copyright © 2008 by Ronald E. Romig
18 Oak Hill Cluster, Independence, Missouri 64057
rromig1@comcast.net

Images, unless otherwise cited, are the copyrighted intellectual property and provided courtesy of Community of Christ Archives, 1001 W. Walnut, Independence, Missouri 64050-3562.

Cover and interior design by John Hamer
Typesetting by Ronald E. Romig
Copyediting by Lavina Fielding Anderson
Special thanks to Ardis Parshall, Anne Romig, and Rene Romig for proofing and copyediting selected documents.

Editorial method: Original spelling and punctuation maintained. Editorial comments in brackets. Strikethroughs eliminated. Insertions shown in <->.

FRONT COVER IMAGE: David H. Smith painting of the Nauvoo House on the Mississippi River, ca. 1868. Left to right: David H. Smith, the painter, Emma Smith Bidamon. Image used by permission of the Community of Christ Archives and the Lynn Smith Family.

BACK COVER IMAGE: Emma and David Hyrum Smith, ca. 1845.

Table *of* Contents

Special thanks to the following for the use of materials:

Joy Goodwin, Emma crossing the Mississippi

The Huntington Library, Julia Murdock Smith Dixon Middleton letters

LDS Church Library, letters, documents and photographs

Bill Shepard, Elisha Dixon Nauvoo Mansion advertisement

Dover Sindelar and Reed Murdock, photograph of Julia

Lynn Smith Family, David Smith paintings

Dr. Clarendon E. Van Norman Jr., via. Rick Grunder, John Middleton photograph

Emma's Family

Biography of Emma Hale Smith Bidamon

From Inez A. Kennedy, *Recollections of the Pioneers of Lee County, Illinois*, 1893

IN ANTICIPATION OF the publication of a history of Lee County, Illinois, Joseph Smith III provided many intimate details of the life of his mother Emma to Mrs. D. C. Chase, of Amboy. A substantial part of the resultant biographical sketch of Emma, deals with the arrest of her husband Joseph during a visit at the home of Emma's sister, Elizabeth Wasson, in Dixon, Lee County, Illinois. While this essay contains obvious errors, it affords reavealing glimpses of Emma's life of which only members of the family would have knowledge.

Emma Hale Smith Bidamon

EMMA HALE, THE sister of Elizabeth Wasson, was born in the town of Harmony, Susquehanna county, Pennsylvania, July 10, 1804. Her parents, Mr. Isaac and Mrs. Elizabeth (Lewis) Hale, were pioneers of self-reliant race, brave, honest, of unshaken fidelity and unquestioned integrity. She grew to womanhood amid the rural scenes, labors and recreations incident to farm life on the banks of the Susquehanna River. She was a good horse-woman, and a canoe on the river was her plaything. She was a fair scholar for the common schools of the time, and a good singer and possessed of a fine voice. She was of excellent form, straight and above medium height, features strongly marked, hair and eyes brown, while her general intelligence and fearless integrity, united with her kindness of heart and splendid physical developments commanded both admiration and respect.

In 1825 Miss Hale became acquainted with Joseph Smith, celebrated in the history of the religions of the United States, as the founder of "Mormonism," "The Church of Jesus Christ of Latter Day Saints," to whom she was married in the town of South Bainbridge, New York, at the residence of Squire Tarbell, January 18, 1827. Mrs. Smith lived in the family of her husband's parents, at Manchester, New York, until December, when they moved to Harmony, Pennsylvania, and settled near her father's farm.

Joseph and Emma Smith home, Harmony, Pennsylvania, 1903, courtesy LDS Church Library

In September of this year, Mr. Smith became possessed of the plates from which he is said to have written the "Book of Mormon." These plates Mr. Smith had during their residence in their home near Isaac Hale, and of them Mrs. Smith states:

"I knew that he had them. I made a linen sack for Mr. Smith to carry them in. They lay on a stand in my room, day after day, for weeks at a time, and I often moved them in cleaning the room and dusting the table. They were of metal, and when thumbed, as one sometimes thumbs the leaves of a book, would give off a metallic sound."

[The following reminiscence conflates Joseph Smith's treasure-seeking experience at Harmony, Pennsylvania, and the account of finding gold plates near Palmyra, New York.]

A gentleman, now a resident of Amboy, who was, three or four years ago in business in Binghampton, New York, gives an interesting account of a visit which he made while there to Harmony township, Pennsylvania, where the plates were said, by Mr. Smith to have been found. The historic spot is on the summit of a high hill not far from the Susquehanna river [Manchester Township, New York], and is still visited as a place of interest. The stones which formed the foundations of the derrick used, still surround the deep excavation, which, although partially filled, by the caving in of the earth, is some eighty-five feet deep. A Mr. Benson, whose farm joins the land once owned by Isaac Hale, Mrs. Smith's father, and who was familiar with the early history of both the Hale and Smith families, was the guide and instructor of our informant. Smith was about a year in reaching the depth of a hundred or more feet, where he claimed the Angel Moroni had made known to him the plates were to be found. He, with some of his friends, would work at the place until the money gave out, when the work must wait until more means to carry it on were obtained. One enthusiastic follower spent his farm and beggared himself in the search for the hidden treasure. Some people thought Smith insane, but his preaching drew to him crowds of followers.

In February, 1829, Mrs. Smith became an amanuensis to her husband, and from his dictation she wrote much of the celebrated Book of Mormon; and in this year it was completed and published in Palmyra, New York, by E. B. Grandin. It was in this year that Oliver Cowdery joined his fortune and influence with the new movement begun by Joseph Smith.

The persecutions which followed now compelled a removal from Harmony. And in August, 1830, the family moved to Fayette, Seneca county, New York. From here, in January, 1831, they went to Kirtland, Ohio, where Newel K. Whitney, one of the leading men in the Mormon society, befriended them. The sickness incidental to a new country prevailed, and Mr. and Mrs. Smith, having lost their first child, adopted a little boy and girl, twin children of Mrs. John Murdock, who died, the father consenting. September, 1831, they moved to Hiram, Portage county, Ohio, thirty-five miles south-east of Kirtland. The converts to Mr. Smith's preaching were constantly arriving from all parts of the country, greatly to the disturbance of antagonists to the Mormon religion, and in March, 1832, the most violent persecution followed. Mr. Smith was dragged

John Johnson house, Hiram, Portage County, Ohio

from his bed, beaten into insensibility, tarred and feathered and left for dead. A strange part of this experience was that his spirit seemed to leave his body, and that during the period of insensibility he consciously stood over his own body, feeling no pain, but seeing and hearing all that transpired.

When, after returning to consciousness, he managed to drag himself back to his home, Mrs. Smith fainted at the sight; and the little adopted boy, who took cold on that fearful night, died the next week. It was a long time, before Mrs. Smith recovered from the shock of all these accumulated sorrows. The same night Sidney Rigdon was subjected to the same treatment.

He [Joseph Smith] now started on a mission to Missouri, Mrs. Smith returning to Kirtland and stopping with her friends, the Whitneys. It is here that Joseph Smith, now of Lamoni, Decatur county, Iowa, was born, November 6, 1832.

In April, 1838, the family moved to Missouri, in Caldwell county. Here Mrs. Smith hoped for the quietude and peace for which she longed, but great numbers of converts flocked to their leader. The people became alarmed and violent persecution which it is useless and painful to detail followed. Accusations of every kind were made, and the extermination of the Mormons seemed to be determined upon. The leaders, Joseph and his brother Hirum [Hyrum] Smith and others were imprisoned, and a summary death from shooting was expected by them. Mrs. Smith was now left with her family of four children; her adopted daughter, her three sons, the oldest six years old, the youngest five months, at the beginning of winter, her husband in jail for his religion's sake, powerless to help him.

What could she do? She bravely visited her husband in the jail, taking her oldest son with her, and while she was permitted but a short interview, she obtained permission to leave the child a guest of his manacled and fettered father, until the next day.

After making such arrangements for the safety of herself and children as she could, Mrs. Smith left the home from which she had been driven, and turned her steps toward Illinois. The winter shut in early, and when the fleeing pilgrims reached the Mississippi River it was frozen over and Mrs. Smith, weary, sad and heart-broken, crossed the mighty river to Quincy, Illinois, on foot, carrying her two youngest children, with the oldest boy and little

Emma crossing the Mississippi River

girl clinging to her dress.

She found a hospitable welcome at the home of a family by the name of Cleveland, where she remained during the long winter, sad, but trusting, and in faithful expectancy, waiting for her husband's relief and delivery from bonds. When, at last, he was free, she welcomed him with a wife's rapture, and was ready to begin again the life of devotion to his happiness as she had ever been.

The little town of Commerce, in Hancock county, Illinois, at the head of the Lower Rapids, had been chosen for a resting place for the refugees, and the family reached it on May tenth. A celebrated river pilot by the name of Hugh White, owned a farm on which was a hewed log house with a clap-board annex, which Mr. Smith bought, and into which he moved his family. Yet, even here, Mrs. Smith knew not what awaited her. All her married life had been such as to call forth the strongest courage and fortitude and faith of her soul, and in none of them had she faltered. What she had and what she was, she had placed on the altar of her devotions; and if God willed, she was content.

The seasons of 1839-40, were seasons of severe trials to the new settlements. Fever incident to the new countries, the long exposure and crying want endured by many in their forced exodus from Missouri, the fogs from the river and miasma from the swamps—all combined to make the season sickly, and hundreds became victims, many of whom died. Mrs. Smith realizing the weight of the general burden and the necessity of proper nursing of the stricken people, opened her house for hospital service. Numbers of the severe cases were removed to her home and placed under her care. She, with her family of children, took shelter in a tent in the dooryard, she, and her children under her direction, doing all that they could to minister to the suffering. At one time she had ten of these unfortunate people in her care, herself and oldest son being the only nurses that were available, the boy doing little except to carry water from the spring near the river's brink to quench the thirst and lave the hands and faces of the fever[-]tried souls.

During a great portion of this trying time, Mrs. Smith's husband was at Washington, D. C., seeking to secure the intervention of the General Government, to obtain an official and final examination of the difficulties between the Mormons and their restless neighbors, and security from the Government in their rights. Mr. Van Buren's answer to their plea when obtained was, "Gentlemen, your cause is just, but I can do nothing for you." Commerce was changed to Nauvoo, the post office department recognizing the change, April 21, 1840.

On June 5, 1841, Joseph was again arrested, as a fugitive from justice, by Sheriff Thomas King, and taken to Monmouth, Illinois, where the case was tried before Judge Stephen A. Douglas, on June 8th. Orville H. Browning, of Quincy, Illinois, afterward Secretary of the Interior under President Lincoln, appearing for the defence [sic]. Mr. Smith was discharged, the judge giving expressions of indignation at the manner the prisoner had been harassed by his persecutors.

On May 6, 1842, Mr. Smith was again arrested, tried at Springfield, and acquitted on proof of innocence.

From this time until about June, 1843, there was a season of rest afforded to the family, which Mrs. Smith was well prepared to enjoy. She was chosen to preside over a society called "The Female Relief Society," formed of prominent women of the large and rapidly increasing city (which had reached a population of 15,000), the object, of the society being to seek out cases of necessity, sickness and distress in the city, to take cognizance of and institute measures for their relief.

Mrs. Smith was chosen to preside because of her well-known probity, clearness of perception, experience and decision of character. This position she held until after the death of her husband, and the dispersion from Nauvoo took place.

Mr. Smith's father died in the fall of 1841, and in the summer of 1842 his mother became a part of his family. Of Mrs. Smith's care of her mother-in-law, that lady herself states: "Soon after I took up my residence at her house I was taken very sick and was brought nigh unto death. For five nights in succession Emma never left me, but stood at my bed-side all night long, at the end of which time she was overcome with fatigue and taken sick herself. Joseph then took her place and watched with me the five succeeding nights as faithfully as Emma had done." From this sickness Mr. Smith's mother soon recovered, but she remained an inmate of the family until her son's death, after which, for some two or three years, she was cared for by her youngest daughter, Lucy Mil[l]iken, and her husband, when she returned to the home of Mrs. Smith, where she remained until May, 1855 [1856], when, in the presence of Mrs. Smith, her grand-son, Joseph, and a neighbor, she passed into the great beyond. This aged mother was confined to her bed, a sufferer from rheumatism,

Lucy Mack Smith

by which her feet, hands and arms were distorted and mis[s]hapen for many years, during the greater part of which time she was provided for and taken care of at the home of Mrs. Smith, the widow of her son, Joseph.

On June 13, 1843, Mrs. Smith, with her husband and children, started by carriage, at that time the only mode of traveling inland, to visit her sister, Mrs. Elizabeth Wasson, the wife of Benjamin Wasson, living in Amboy, Lee county, Illinois. On the same day Gov. Thomas Reynolds, of Missouri, appointed Joseph H. Reynolds, Sheriff of Jackson County, Missouri, to proceed to Illinois with a new writ to operate with Harmon T. Wilson, of Hancock county, Illinois, in arresting Joseph Smith, on a renewal of the same charge from which he

had been discharged by a competent court. These two men followed Mr. Smith to Mr. Wasson's place, which they reached June 23rd, while the family were at dinner. . . ."

Here, as in Missouri, he [Joseph] was taken from the presence of his wife and children without explanation and without opportunity to bid his agitated and tearful wife goodbye. His captors hurried him to Dixon. . . .

As soon as Mr. Smith was arrested, Mrs. Smith determined to reach her home as soon as she could. After ascertaining the course affairs were likely to take at Dixon, under the vigorous regime of Col. Dixon, and Attorneys Patrick and Southwick, Mrs. Smith started with her children for Nauvoo, a young man named Loring [Lorin] Walker driving the team. She reached home some three days before the cavalcade accompanying her husband, and when he and his captors, Sheriff Campbell and the posse reached the city and her home, she was ready to receive them; and notwithstanding there were many to partake at her board, all were amply provided for and treated by her with every mark of kindness, hospitality and respect. The executive ability and energy of Mrs. Smith are demonstrated by the fact that at every stage of her husband's peace, prosperity, peril and distress, she proved equal to the emergency and conducted the affairs of his household, her station in society, and her public appearances, in the calm dignity and conscious rectitude of splendid womanhood. In August, 1843, she became landlady of the Nauvoo Mansion, a hotel quite noted during the last year of Mr. Smith's lifetime and for many years after.

On June 12, 1844, Mr. Smith was again arrested and again dismissed. June 24th Joseph Smith and his brother, Hiram [Hyrum], were again arrested on the charge of treason. After consultation with Gov. Ford and others who advised that they should put themselves into the hands of the civil authorities to answer whatever charges might be made against them, and upon express promise of the governor that they should have a fair and impartial trial, Joseph and Hiram Smith did, on the 24th of June, 1844, proceed to Carthage and presented themselves before him to be taken into custody.

At this interview with the governor he pledged his own faith and that of the State of Illinois, that they should be protected from violence, and have a fair and impartial trial. At dark that night the constable appeared with a mittimus commanding him to commit Joseph and

Emma Smith, sketch by Sutcliffe Maudsley, 1842, courtesy LDS Church Library.

Hiram Smith to jail on a charge of treason against the state, issued by Justice Robert F. Smith. Appeal was made to the governor, but he permitted them to be lodged in jail.

On the morning of the 26th, the governor, at 9:30 o'clock, visited the prison and had a lengthy interview with Joseph and Hiram Smith, in which he was fully informed of what had been done at Nauvoo, and upon which action the charge of treason had been made, and that it was done at the direction of the Governor himself. Governor Ford again gave his pledge that these men should be protected from illegal harm. At 2:30 of the same day, on June 26th, the

Smith brothers were taken by Constable Bettisworth before Justice R. F. Smith to answer for treason, and, on proper showing the trial was adjourned until noon of the 27th, to allow of getting witnesses from Nauvoo, eighteen miles distant.

Afterwards, without notice to defendants, the trial was postponed until the 29th, and the prisoners were remanded to jail.

On the morning of the 27th, Governor Ford and his escort went to Nauvoo. He had disbanded a portion of the state militia, but left the Carthage Grays in charge of the place (Carthage) during his absence, a detail from which body of troops had been stationed as guards at the jail.

Threats had been made openly that the Smiths would not be permitted to leave the town alive. These threats had been made in the hearing of Governor Ford; one Alfred Randall stating that he heard one of the soldiers say to Governor Ford: "The soldiers are determined to see Joe Smith dead before they leave town." The Governor replied, "If you know of any such thing keep it to yourself."

About five o'clock in the afternoon of the same day, June 27, 1844, while Governor Thomas Ford was addressing the citizens of Nauvoo, a mob of armed men, some two hundred strong, disguised by faces blackened, coats turned, and in other ways, approached the jail, a stone and wood building in the south western edge of town, and overpowered the guard, who fired over their heads, killed Joseph and Hiram [sic] Smith, and wounded John Taylor nigh to death. There were in the room, Joseph and Hiram Smith, John Taylor and Willard Richards, the last two named being the only friends of the two men killed whom the officer would allow to stay with them. Each of the men killed and Mr. Taylor were struck by four balls. Hiram Smith fell in the room; Joseph ran to the window and in making an effort to get out was struck by a ball and fell some feet to the ground. The mob, by order of the leader, set his body against a well-curb near the house, and would have fired a volley at it, but he was already dead.

Mr. Richards remained unhurt in the debtor's room where the prisoners had been confined. Their work accomplished the mob retired.

The tragedy was over; the long, long struggle was ended; the loving wife who had been faithful through all things for "better or worse," had only to wait in tearless woe the last home coming of him with whom she had plighted her faith for seventeen years.

In the afternoon of the 28th the bodies of the two men were brought home to their grief[-]stricken families and friends. The long pending stroke had fallen, and Mrs. Smith was a widow with a family of four children, the eldest thirteen. She shed few tears, but in stony[-]eyed, silent grief bore her trial, and waited until thousands had passed the bier on which her dead was lying, when, with her children by her, she sat down by the silent form. "My husband, O, my husband! Have they taken you from me at last?" That night she parted from her only steadfast, earthly friend, and began the singular life of patient endurance and self-denial to which his death subjected her.

An administrator was appointed to take charge of Mr. Smith's estate. That it was not large may be known by the fact, that with the usual widow redemption the sum of $124.00 per year was allowed her for the care of herself and family. A number of creditors appeared, and what property there was left became the prey of the creditors and the legal costs, so that, by the time the estate was settled, it gave Mrs. Smith a few lots with their buildings in the town of Nauvoo, and some acres of land lying in the country. With this, and patient industry, she set herself to the task of rearing her family, which

on the 17th of the next November after her husband's death, was increased by the birth of a son, whom she called David Hirum [Hyrum], for her brother David and her husband's brother.

The troubles between the people of the adjoining counties and the Mormon people culminated in the expulsion of the latter from the state. Mrs. Smith had, by her opposition to the measures and policy of President Brigham Young, become obnoxious to him, and to those who accepted him, so that when in the fall and early winter of 1846 the Latter Day Saints left the state, she, ostensibly one of them, and yet opposed to their policy, was included in this extradition. Determined not to be compromised with evil and its consequences, Mrs. Smith, to avoid possible insult, if not injury from the anti-Mormon forces when they should enter the city according to the terms of capitulation, left Nauvoo with her family on board the steamer "Uncle Toby," Captain Grimes, commander, on the 12th day of September, 1846, for Fulton City, Whiteside county, Illinois, whither one of her friends, William Marks, had preceded her. She was accompanied by parts of four other families, whom she took under her guidance and care. Wesley Knight and family, Loring Walker (who had married a daughter of Hiram Smith) and his family, two orphan girls, (Angeline and Nancy Carter), and a young man by the name of William Clapp. Mrs. Smith remained at Fulton City until February, when, learning that the man whom she had left in possession of her hotel was going to dismantle the house and embark for Texas with the spoils, she made the trip by carriage to Nauvoo, which she reached in the afternoon of February 19, 1847, and so determinedly pushed her claims, that in three days she was again installed in her house as its mistress.

Mrs. Smith nobly and faithfully fulfilled a mother's duties for her children until by marriage and death they left her. She continued to live in Nauvoo until her death, April 30, 1879. Her last words were, as looking upward, with feeble arms outstretched toward some one whom she seemed to see, "Yes, yes, I am coming."

She became a member of the church over which her husband presided in June, 1830, and remained always in the faith she then embraced, so that when at Amboy, Illinois, in 1860, her son joined the Reorganized or Anti-polygamous branch of the so-called Mormon church, she was with him, and also united with that church. In that faith she lived;

Emma Smith Bidamon, ca. 1870s

in it she died, undeviatingly devoted and faithful.

The life of this rare woman was passed in a remarkable period of our Nation's history. The same firmness, and independence, love of right and hatred of wrong, which characterized her sister, Mrs. Wasson, and others of her family, also characterized her. . . . She was patient and just with her children, reared her four sons to manhood, to honor and revere her name. . . . She had the courage of her convictions, she hated tyranny and oppression, and her sons inherited from her the same spirit. . . .

—Inez A. Kennedy, *Recollections of the Pioneers of Lee County* (Dixon, Illinois: Inez A. Kennedy, Publisher, 1893), 96-107.

Emma's Family Correspondence

EMMA HALE SMITH Bidamon left very little in writing as a reflection of her interesting life. Apparently, Emma allowed little time for such reflection. Her life was devoted to caring for those around her. Her home was always full of visitors while married to Joseph Smith. As mistress of the Nauvoo Mansion House, Emma attended to countless visitors.

After Joseph's death, Emma worked tirelessly providing for her family. Continuing to operate the Nauvoo Mansion, she furnished room and board to innumerable people.

Happily, Emma's correspondence with her family is a notable exception to her limited writing. As her children grew to adulthood and began families, Emma kept in touch via letters.

Emma's Family is a documentary history, offering minimal introductory context or historical interpretation. Emma's correspondence to and from her family speaks for itself.

Original spelling and punctuation in the documents that follow are maintained.

Lewis Crum Bidamon

Biography of Lewis Crum Bidamon

LEWIS BIDAMON'S father, Dedrich Bidamon (also known as John Dedrich), was born in Pennsylvania prior to 1765. Dedrich Bidamon is believed to be the son or grandson of Dietrich Bidelman who emigrated from the Palatinate area of Germany arriving in Philadelphia on 31 August 1730. The first Dedrich settled in Philadelphia and later moved to Berks County, Pennsylvania.

Lewis's mother, Mary Crum was also born in Pennsylvania in 1779. After Dedrich's and Mary's marriage, the newlyweds apparently settled in western Virginia, (now West Virginia) where their son Lewis Crum Bidamon was born in 1802. Lewis's family is enumerated in the Smithfield Township, Jefferson County, Ohio, census of 1810, where they lived until sometime after 1814. The family next moved to Highland County, Ohio, and purchased land. This move took place prior to February 1819. The family consisted of brothers John Crane, Christian, and Frederick, and sisters Rosannah, Mary Sarah, Elizabeth, and Nancy. At some point, Lewis's mother Mary died. Around 1824-25, Lewis married Nancy Sebree of Pickaway County, Ohio. In 1830, they were living in Williamsport, Deer Creek Township, Pickaway County, Ohio. A son under five also appears in the 1830 census.

Lewis and family, along with Nancy's family, made the overland trek from Ohio to Fulton County, Illinois, arriving in Canton by horse and wagon October 1832. Lewis's and Nancy's daughter Zerelda Ann was born while the family was living in Canton in 1834. Another daughter, Mary Elizabeth, was born between 1835 and 1840.

In 1833, Lewis constructed the first house on the Canton public square and was active in the affairs of the city. Lewis ran for the office of trustee in 1838. Sometime prior to 1843 he purchased the Ellis Steam Mill in Canton, converting it into a foundry which he operated until 1846. During this period, he and his brother John apparently had business contacts with Joseph Smith in the manufacture of wagons for carriages and became familiar with Nauvoo. After Rigdon's departure, Lewis's brother John supposedly bought Sidney Ridgon's house. This transaction apparently occurred in late 1844 or early 1845; the price was $600.

During the "Mormon War" in September 1846, Bidamon carried a message from Illinois Governor Ford to Canton, Illinois for Major J. R. Parker. Bidamon handed Parker his commission along with instructions to recruit a force and proceed to Nauvoo. This is the first documented instance of the title "Major" being applied to Bidamon; beyond this, the origin of the title or commission has not been found.

According to Linda Newell's and Valeen Avery's book, *Mormon Enigma*, Bidamon's wife Nancy and son died prior to 1847. Bidamon's daughter Mary Elizabeth married early, and Zerelda Ann, thirteen years old in 1847, was still living in Canton. By this time, Bidamon was living in Nauvoo and met Emma Smith in the spring of 1847. A relationship developed and Lewis Bidamon and Emma Smith were married on 23 December 1847.

On or about 1 May 1849, L. C. and brother John left Nauvoo via the overland route for the California gold fields. Surviving correspondence describes the hardships and trials of the trail. Bidamon returned home late in 1850 via the Panama Canal, Cuba, and the Mississippi River. John remained in California where he became sheriff of Placerville. Whatever gold Lewis found in California was lost by the time he returned home.

In 1862, L. C. had a son Charles E., born to Mary Abercrombie, a widow living with her three children on the Daniel and Thomas Luce farm. When Charley was about seven years old, Lewis brought his son to live with him.

As described in *Mormon Enigma*, Lewis participated in the Civil War in 1862 with the Illinois State Militia, reportedly serving with the 32nd Regiment. After duty on the front, Lewis returned home in May or June of 1865.

L. C. and Emma continued their life together, and in 1869 the Major rebuilt the Nauvoo House hotel on part of its original foundation and the couple occupied the structure following construction. Emma died in April 1879. In keeping with Emma's wish, L. C. married Nancy Abercrombie on 20 May 1880.

Major Lewis Crum Bidamon died on 11 February 1891 and is buried across the street from the Nauvoo House in the Smith Family burial ground in the yard of the old Smith homestead.

—Based on Edward A. Luce, "The Bidamon Story," MS 7459, f2, items 5, 6, LDS Church Library.

Correspondence *with*
Lewis Bidamon

EMMA'S EARLIEST correspondence with Lewis Bidamon included a business transaction.

LEWIS BIDAMON, letter to Emma Smith:

Canton Fulton Co Ills
Jany 11th 1847

Dear Madam

I Wright to you from this place where I have bin ever Since our defeat at Nauvoo I was taken sick shortley after I arived here with the Bilious Fever allmost dispared of recovery by my physician and Friends My recoverry is verry Slow I am onley now able to walk about the House My Brother John and Famley have mooved back and I Shall returene assoon as my helth will admit of Traveling They tell me ther is nothing but peace and tranquility ther existing—My Brother Frederick and Fameley are now living in this place they all came from Galena sick with the Fever & agu

NB Brother John and my self are desireous to Rent the Mansion House of you if you intend leting it

and if So pleas inform me what will be your Termes per annum we wish to Rent House Barne and Furnature infine evry thing that pertains to the Tavern Pleas excuse this billit I am verry nervis

Your Cincere Friend and wel Wisher Lewis Bidamon

—Lewis Bidamon, letter to Emma Smith, 11 January 1847, Emma Smith Papers, P4, f28, CofC Archives.

Lewis Crum Bidamon, courtesy Liberty Hall, Lamoni, Iowa

Emma Smith Daguerreotype of 1844 Oil Portrait

Daguerrian photograph of painting of Emma Smith, by David Rogers, at Nauvoo, Illinois, in September 1842.

Family Heirloom

EMMA SMITH, letter to Lewis Bidamon:

January 1847

Mr Bidamon

Yours of the 11th Jany came to [me] was received yesterday, in answer to which I have to say, that I suppose I shall have to get possesion of the Mansion before I can rent it again, as I do not expect You would like to rent it and run the risk of geting possesion as I do not know as Dr. Van T will be wiling to give up the property he has in his posesion indeed I do expect Some trouble with him yet before I get out of [it] through if your Brother is in Nauvoo perhaps he can find out on what conditions he will give up posesion of the premises I e[x]pect that I shall be like to know what I am to depend upon about the first of March. I want to rent the farm that is near Na[uvoo]. If you know of some one that wishes to rent it you would do me a favour to let me know of it. Upland I have another farm between the Quincy roade and Warsaw near Marshes that I wish to rent or sell I also have a number of City lots in Na[uvoo] I would like to sell. I am anxiously waiting to know what our new Gov is agoing to do with regard to the affairs of Hancock.

I formed a very aggreabl acquaintince with your brothers Fr. [Frederick's] family while on the boat with them and would be pleased to see them again and that too under more pleasant circumstances. You will please give them my best respects

Yours Truly, [Emma Smith]

—Emma Smith, letter to Lewis Bidamon, [January 1847], Emma Smith Papers, P4, f28, CofC Archives.

Emma Smith, letter to Lewis Bidamon, January 1847

MMA'S AND LEWIS'S BUSINESS ACQUAINTANCE blossomed into a personal relationship. On December 23, 1847, Emma Smith and Major Lewis Bidamon were married by Methodist Minister William Haney.

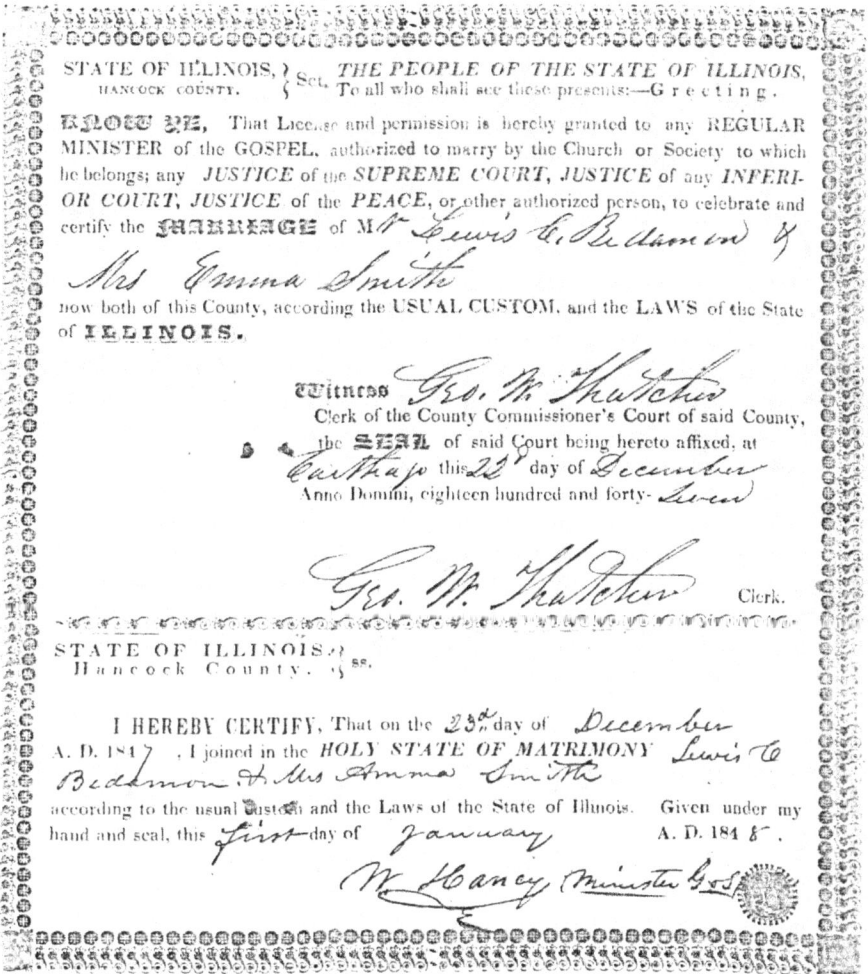

STATE OF ILLINOIS, } Set. THE PEOPLE OF THE STATE OF ILLINOIS,
HANCOCK COUNTY. To all who shall see these presents:—G r e e t i n g .

KNOW YE, That License and permission is hereby granted to any REGULAR MINISTER of the GOSPEL, authorized to marry by the Church or Society to which he belongs; any JUSTICE of the SUPREME COURT, JUSTICE of any INFERIOR COURT, JUSTICE of the PEACE, or other authorized person, to celebrate and certify the MARRIAGE of Mr *Lewis C. Bidamon* & *Mrs Emma Smith* now both of this County, according the USUAL CUSTOM, and the LAWS of the State of ILLINOIS.

Witness *Geo. W. Thatcher*
Clerk of the County Commissioner's Court of said County, the SEAL of said Court being hereto affixed, at *Carthage* this *22* day of *December* Anno Domini, eighteen hundred and forty- *Seven*

Geo. W. Thatcher Clerk.

STATE OF ILLINOIS } ss.
Hancock County.

I HEREBY CERTIFY, That on the *23d* day of *December* A. D. 1847 , I joined in the HOLY STATE OF MATRIMONY *Lewis C Bidamon & Mrs Emma Smith* according to the usual custom and the Laws of the State of Illinois. Given under my hand and seal, this *first* day of *January,* A. D. 184 8 .

W. Haney, minister Gospel

Emma Smith and Lewis Bidamon marriage certificate,
courtesy LDS Church Library, MS 7461.

IN 1849, WHEN NEWS of the discovery of gold in California reached Nauvoo, Lewis Bidamon headed for the gold fields.

Lewis C. Bidamon, letter to Emma Smith Bidamon:

Canesvill[e], [Iowa,]
May 21st 1849

My Dear Emma

I address you from this place where We arived on the 19th inst all well and no accident happened worthy of note, I recd you[r] Letter at the hand of Bobbit on the prarie 40 miles from this place the verry thoughts of receving it comeing from your hands was a sorse of plesure

we find maney emigrants bound for Califonia which I fear will render feed verry Scarce we are agoing to organise a company to day and will probley Cross the river tomorrow

the Mormons receive us verry kindly and appear to feel a deep intrust in your wellfare

you stated in your letter that you thought it expedient to give more quitclames [quitclaims] I leave that to your good Jugment and accompaney this with a power of attorney to M M Morrill to Sine my name to any p[r]ofer of the kind. The gold news is Still increesing and more flattering the farther west we get,

the attraction is powerfull both east and west the gold on the one hand and my Dear Emma on the other the cost has the preeminence but duty Sais press West O Emma that I could even have the prevolage of your Society as long as I am penning theas reflections I would hold it pricless but why Should I greeve fate has ordered it So my Love be cherefull and content I will doo the best I Can and will return as Soon as I Can to press you to my now akeing brest fare you well untill you here from me again or See me

I remane your affectionate Husband untill death L C Bidamon

NB let me here from you whene ever there is a chance.

Give my Love to all the Children tell Zerelda to be a good and obedient girl My respects to my friends My Curses to my enemeys Phylindy John is well he will nodoubt right to you

May 23rd

We did not get of[f] as we expected in concequence of Ivy Owns not ariving as we expected he has not yet arived but we have heard from him he will be here today but we roll on this morning

a Mr McCaslin Strove hard to give me trouble on a order that calls for $45 which bares Emma Smiths Signature dated May 1843 he put it

in the hands of the officers for collection but Georg A Smith is my
friend and Mr McCaslin is defeated
LCB

—Lewis C. Bidamon, letter
to Emma Smith Bidamon, 21 May
1849, Miscellaneous Collection,
P87, f5, CofC Archives.

Emma *and* David H. Smith Daguerreotype, 1844

Family Heirloom

EMMA REMAINED in Nauvoo, caring for the family and operating the Mansion House hotel.

LEWIS C. BIDAMON, letter to Emma Smith Bidamon:

Indian Territory July 5th 1849
My Dear Wife

I address you from this point after a tedious travell over the black hills or rather barren mountains and once burning volcanoes we past for miles over earth and stones throwed in hetrogenous mases resembling Spanish brown it looks as though our cattle would Starve though at this place at the crosing at deer creek 1020 miles from Nauvoo the prospect for gras appears Some better but knownot how it will hold out we find no grass near the road we are often obliged to drive our stock to the distanc of 4 miles up the ravveenes for feed the cattle Stand the jant better than the mules and horses we have past maney mule tranes. As it respects helth we have bin Severely thretened with the Cholary John and I have both had Strong Simptems and was verry Sick but are now well and Injoy good helth Nathan King has enjoyed excellent helth all the time report Sais there has bin 500 deaths

on the differant routs from the Mosuria Rivver to this plaece though we have Lost but three out of our companey and the ballance [are] at presant well, On the night of the 4th Some 300 of us met and had quite a Jubelee had a cow Tilion [cotillion] or an tilion on the plat flat Speaches & etsetry and 1200 gunes the Knoxvill and Canton trains cattle took a Stampeed on the loop fork of plat they lost 46 head of their cattle which they have never found at this place they asked us $3.50 cts. for ferrying each Wagon we would not pay it but bot 4 canoes lashed them to gather ferryed our train over and ferryed others to the amt of $50 and Sold the Boat for what it cost us

we have seen but few Indians they were fifteen hundred formed a line across the road and Stoped a train of Califonians and told them they Should not go any further they were bringing a diseas in their contry that killed their people

the Train stoped untill other Trains drove up armed them Selfs formed a line of battle and marched towards the Indians, they gathered up their packs in doble quick time and crost the plat and but verry few Indians have bin Seen Since

Dear Emma ofttimes me mind hovers around the[e] and in amagination press the[e] tenderly to my bosom

O my Love if I could onley here from you and know that you was well and the family and you was injoying your Selfs it would ease this akeing hart it would over compare with the briliant prospects of my Success in Califonia Be cherefull Dear, if we live the day will arive when we will again meet and press each other to our congenios brests fare you well for the present

L. C. Bidamon

July 16th

I againe find lesure to Wright.

We are this evning camped on the east Bank of Sweet watter River though we have crost it 4 times we are now within 40 miles of the South pass. The grass is litterally eaten out and if we donot find better feed our Stock must Starve to death though we hope for the better, all the grass that grows here is along the river on bottemns from 50 yds to one mile wide and the cattle of 6000 Waggons to feed on. The emigrants are kind and peaceable towards eacother I find many warme friends on the rout We are amongst the Spurs of the Rocky Mountain they are nothing but massive piles of granet rock and the planes nothing but Sand and gravel and [n]aught but wild Sage that grow on them This day we took Some boutiful Ice from the marsh 2 feet below the terf it was verry acceptable. I must not forget to tell you I have become acquainted with Mr. Rae your old Bough the Editor I forget the name of the paper in the East he made a presant of a pare of gumelastick Boots to me which reaches to my but[t] he appears verry kind and fermilar he is on his way to California The acount from the gold Regeans is good and I think we will do well if we Should be so lucky as to get there I have not Seen or heard a word of Mr Wasson Since he left Nauvoo We have not had any rain Since the first of Juny but almost constant winds and hot

days & cold nights We have throwe away Something like 1000 lbs of our loading and reduced the wate of our Wagon all we can and walk all we are able to and yet it is dificult to get through the Sands the _ [right side of page is torn away for the rest of the letter and will be indicated by _] are nothing yet compared to the Sands

August 16th 1849
Goos Creek Calafonia

We are now 16 hundred & 40 miles from _N[auvoo]_ 600 & 20 miles from our destination

I intended sending this sheet by Babit bu[t] _[I]_ faled meeting him I now send it by a man _[from]_ Salt Lake when you will get it I know _[not]_ our prospect for geting to the gold regions _[looks]_ more faverable than when I rote the abov[e]

we are all well and in good spirrits I am now Siting in the grass and the wind _[blows]_ So I cant Spell let lone Wright, it is useles[s] for me to give you a hist[o]ry of our jorn[ey] Suffice it to say we have past through the[valley] of death I will returne as soon as I _[can]_ and then will take pleasure in ac[counting] our hole trip   L. C. Bidamon

—Lewis Crum Bidamon, Letter to Emma Smith Bidamon, 5 July, 16 July, and 16 August 1849, Lewis C. Bidamon Papers, P12-2, f13, CofC Archives.

Major Lewis Crum Bidamon, ca. 1860s.

David H. Smith Sketch *of the* Homestead, ca. 1868

Emma tended to farm duties during Bidamon's absence,
sketch of Homestead, by David H. Smith

Emma Smith Bidamon, ca. 1875

EMMA SMITH Bidamon, letter to Lewis C. Bidamon:

Nauvoo, Jan. the 7 1850
My ever dear Husband

It was with feelings I cannot describe that I received a letter on the 29th of Dec. bearing the hand writing that I know so well and hastened to my chamber to enjoy its Contents, which my Selfish feelings led me to believe belonged to me first, and the satisfaction I enjoyed in perusing that letter none ever knew, or ever will know, but the truly faithful heart, that has waited in anxious suspence as long as I had, but it was your handwriting, and I knew that you yet lived and remembered me. I was not only glad, but very thankfull to a kind providence that you had been blessed with So much health and prosperity, through your long and tedious journey. My dear Lewis I have scarsley enjoyed any good thing since you left home, in consequence of the constant terifying apprehension that you might be suffering for the most common comforts of life. I never have been weary without thinking that you might be much more so. I never have felt the want of food without fearing that you might be almost, or quite starving, and I have never been thirsty without feeling my heart Sicken with the reflection that perhaps you was sinking, faint, and famished for want of that reviving draught that I could obtain So easy, and use So freely, and I very much feared that the heat of the Sun on those burning plains, might Seriously affect you, but now those anxieties are over, and some may think that I might be Content, but I am not, neither can I be untill you are within my grasp, then, and not till then shall I be free from fears for your Safety, and anxieties for your wellfare I have written three letters and directed them to San Francisco, and one that I sent by Mr. Webster directed to Sacramento, in all of which I wrote the most important buisness transactions, but I fear you will never get them, and if you should you will find nearly all that I could tell you now about our affairs. and Mr. Morrill has promised to write a long letter to you and John and let you know how Some particular matters Stand, and if he does it will be done much better than I could do it if I should try.

Morrill and McLennan disolved [sic] partnership last fall, and Mc and Frank Hall have gone to the Bluffs with a stock of Goods this winter to try their luck there. Perhaps John can guess how they will make out. I will repeat in this letter some that I wrote in my former letters, and among the most important items are the following. Mary E was maried to a Mr. Gleason on the 30 of last July I think. She came out here the same week, and Zarelda went back with them, and I have not heard one word from them Since. We did not have the Cholera here last summer. I never knew a more healthy year in this place but it may be here this season as I learned it is already in St. Louis, but if it is as many think, that the reason the Cholera was not here was because there was no St Bt [Steam Boat] landing here we shall be as safe from it as we were last year, for there was not enough done on the wharf to make the landing any better than it was before it was commenced. I earnestly hope that the allwise ruler of

Heaven will remmember that those beings that are in this place who would be humane if they had half a chance, has enough to contend with, without having the scourge of Nations Sent among them, it is imposible to give You an idea of the gloomy Solitude that reigned here last year after You left home.

The Cholera frightened the people out of traveling unless they were positively oblidged to and we were left with Mr. Eliotte alone as a boarder, and he would have gone if he had not been afraid to, and after setting up our accounts and paying Esq. Williams his fees, I found myself unable to furnish the nessesary requitsites to keep up the Mansion, and I was convinced by the circumstances that I had better let Dixon take it as the Cholera prevented him from staying in St. Louis where he got into buisness at forty dollars a month and was found everything, he done better than I expected, as he expended about one hundred dollars preparing the house, but the buisness and climate did not agree with his broken constitution, and his Physicians told him he must go south or not live till Spring, accordingly he started about the 10th of Dec for Cuba, but only got to St. Louis where he had been confined to his bed for three weeks. This is the last news we have had yet of

IN 1848, JULIA MARRIED Elisha Dixon who took over management of the Mansion.

Nauvoo Mansion.
Main Street, Nauvoo, Illinois.

THE SUBSCRIBER respectfully announces to his friends and the public in general, that he has taken the above commodious and well known Hotel; which has recently undergone a thorough repair, and with new furniture, etc. He is ready to accommodate the traveler and citizen in a superior style. Having had much experience in the above business, and with the facilities that this market affords for providing his table, and a strict attention to business, he feels confident in saying that entire satisfaction will be given to all those who may favor him with their patronage.

☞ There cannot be found a more healthy or pleasant location in the Mississippi valley to spend the summer months, it being a fine situation of country for hunting, and the river at this place abounds with the finest of fish. One of the largest and best arranged Stables in the Western country is connected with the House—a careful and competent Ostler always in attendance. Nauvoo, June 6, 1849, E. Dixon.

—*Valley Whig & Keokuk Registry* 8 (21 June 1849).

UNFORTUNATELY, Dixon's health failed and he left Nauvoo abruptly.

him, it is posible that he may get his health, but I have no idea he will. Julia is with me and is almost as lonely as I am.

It is rather lean keeping tavern when we have but two or three boarders and the Post Office is kept on the hill so that there is no mail stops here, but we have sometimes one or two strangers stop here in the course of a week. if buisness is no better here in the Spring than it was last I think I shall take the Sign down, and do all we can on the farm. Now my dear do not think I am Complaining, as I do not Complain of any thing but the treacherous designing knavery of a pack of cut throat Swindlers as there is Congregated here.

I have been trying to Save some property but I can assure you that my Chance of saving property is just as good as a woman's Chance would be in the fifth Story of a burning building in Broad Way N.Y. when You might see her standing in the front window holding her most presious goods in her hands, hesitating whether to throw her goods back into the flames, or throw them into the streets among the thieves. Now You must not be Surprised if in Such a dilemma I should throw some into the fire and some into the hands of thieves, for it is imposible for me to know and fore know everything, and if in spite of all the combinations of lazy lawyers, and treacherous hypocrites, I do Succeede in saving enough Soil to rais our corn and potatoes on I do believe that You in the goodness of Your generous soul will say that I have not done as bad as I might, for I think there is Some in the world that would not have Stuck to the turf here as long as I have but you may rest assured that I Shall do the best I Can.

There is much more that I intended to write but have not time now but I expect Morrill will write all the most important items of our buisness and Mr. Eliotte has promised to write You all the general news of the day but just told me not to forget to give You his best and warmest respects, and the Children all want you to know that they still remember and still respect You, indeed I believe it would have done Your Soul good if you could have Seen how anxious they were to know if You were well and then Joseph and Frederick, and Alexander were not satisfied till they had all read Your letter, and Joseph Coppied it imediately for Mary Elizabeth.

Since I got Your Sacramento letter I have received one from you dated 5th of July, and post marked at Salt Lake the 11 of October, and I guess that it is or will be a mystery to you how your letter come to go to the Salt Lake when your letter wrote at the same time was mailed at Kanesvill and come directly through, but I cannot come to any other Conclusions than that the Mormons thought best to have Your letter examined, and perhaps Coppied before I had the pleasure of reading it. My dear Lewis You cannot realize how thankful I was when I learned that You had got from the Bluffs safe and did not go by the valley. I want you should be particularly Cautious of those Mormons for I believe they intend that I shall not enjoy anything without trial. Perhaps you do not need any Caution from me. You might have seen enough to convince you that their intentions are any thing but good, yet I must say again keep a good wash [watch] towards them, it may seem strange and ungrateful to You that they should even wish you harmed, and so it is, but I can tell you they are Capable of as infamous ingratitude as any other beings. All that I Can find that they have against You is they think that you occupy a Situation here that you have no buisness to. This is what Babbit told me himself the day before he started from here. You will understand what that means better by Saying it as explained by Babbit that you had no right to marry me, and of Course on the same principle I had no right to marry You. I was told Concerning Some proposals made by the Ms [Mormons] to You, and Your answers to them about Your Coming back to get me to go to the valley. I think You manged very prudently. I hope you will Continue so to do, but when O! when Can I begin to think about your Coming home. I shall expect another welcome letter next month and shall write in season to have my letters always ready for the Monthly packet from N.O. No more at present only that I am as ever yours wholy

Emma Bidamon

David often wishes it was not so far to Sacramento he thinks that he will be very tired of traveling before he gets home. He is by me now and says he loves his pa because he promised to bring him some gold in a little box and he is going to love him till he gets home.

—Emma Smith Bidamon, letter to Lewis C. Bidamon, 7 January 1850, Emma Smith Papers, P4, f30, CofC Archives.

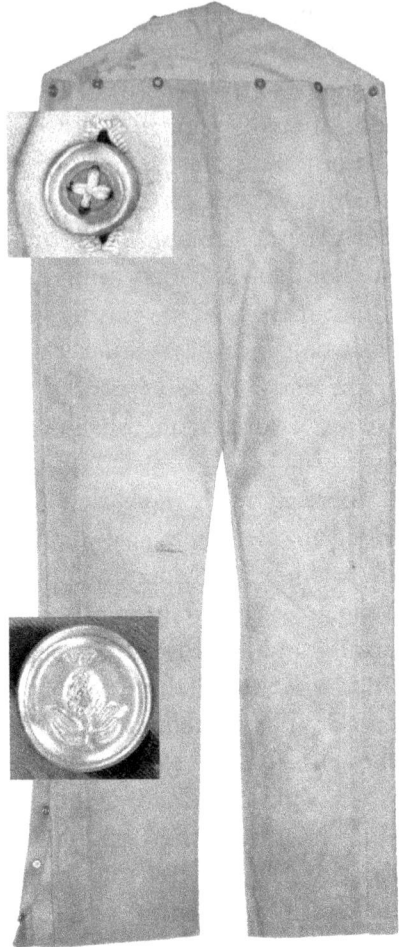

Lewis Bidamon's trousers, believed to have been made by Emma, showing detail of bone and brass buttons. Original housed at Communty of Christ Museum, Independence, Missouri

Sam Brannan's store and hotel, Sacramento, California, 1849, pen and ink drawing by Emanuel Wyttenbach, Courtesy of the California History Room, California State Library, Sacramento, California.

LEWIS C. BIDAMON, letter to Emma:

California Lot 37 30 m
Apr 20th 1850

My Dearley beloved and affectionate Companion

Tong [tongue] cannot express the hapiness I experianced in the anouncement of your letter by the barer thereof to our Tent which is Situated about 100 miles (South east) from Sacremento City and O the extacie of Joy in the perrusial thereof finding you alive and well and the famley enjoy good helth I had allmost concluded that you existed not, and my friends if I had any had forgotten such beeing as I lived but thank Heaven there is one Dear Sullenary [solitary] Angel Still bares me in mind O my Dear Emma that I could press you to my lonesom Hart and converce with you as long as I am pening my feelings I would be in a maner contented untill my set time to returne which will be I think between the last of October and the first of December after that the antisipation or the partisipation of emence welth Shall not keep me from your Dear imbraces untill then my Love try to be content and happy, greeve not if the infamous deemons Should filch all of your property they cannot destroy our Love and if we are blest with helth and Strength we can live happy God will protect the noble in Hart, Gold is not as easy obtained nor in Such abundance in Califonia as was and is antisipated by the people of the States it is obtained by the hardest of labour harder than my constitution is able to bare. the acquasition of gold in the mines is Something like a loterry there is Sometimes large amts obtained in a Short time and with but little labour but these are few occurrences and fare betwen, the most that John and I have dug in a day is $30 and as low as five, and many days not any thing, we cannot work as hard here as we could in the States, it must be in concequenc of being deprived of good and holesom dyet. our living consists of in general, often Sour Flour bread pickled pork venisin or beef and not fat at that, and Scarcley ever any kind of vegitables and especly in the mountains where we are. The prices of provision are as follows or was in the Winter in the mines, as fare out from the city as 50 miles Flour 100 cts pickled pork 100 beenes 75 Coffee 100 Saleratus 600 potatoes 100 Sugar 100 onions 100 Dryed apples 150 peaches 200 fresh Beef from 38 to 50 fresh pork 100 Lard 100 butter 250 Chese 100 Corne meal 75 per pound those prices are any number

of pounds under 50 and verry little demunition in prices above that amt of pounds molasses $8.00 vinegar $4 pr gallon Ardent Sperrits $4 pr qrt mules from 140 to 300 Dollars a peace Liquor pr Drink 50 cts we are tolerably temperate Corse Boots from 30 to 75 dollars pr pare Corse Shoes from 5 to 8 Dollars and evry thing else in propotion I had liken to forgot to tell you the price of Eggs, from 6 to 12 Dollars pr dosin It is but Little Eggnog and Custard that we use here

I received the Letter that Babit carried in May and amswered [answered] it and enclosed a power of attorney at Council Bluff and one on the [__] night of the 19th May 1850 which cawses me to Spend the 20th so plasently these are all the Letters that I have received from your precious Hands Since I last Saw you

I have Written 5 Letters for you as follow one at Drake Vale Iowa Canes vill Iowa one at Ft Laramey and commenced one at Deer Creek but did not finish it untill we got to Goos Creek Some 1100 miles from home and there left it with a verry Clever Morman in apparence by the name if I recollect aright of Willice who promised that the Letter Should be maled at Salt Lake City which I think is the one that you thought was Sent from C Bluffs one at Sacremento and one at Dry Creek Mines Sometime in January which is the last, with this exciption We are dooing but little for the presant

last february the weather appeared So nice and pleasant we thought the Winter was over and not contented with the mines in that Section concluded to go Higher in the mountains concqently packed Some few things on Some mules and arived here where we have found Winter ever cence and but verry pore digings, but we have a prospect that appears some what flatering about 25 miles further in the mountains where it is Low there are pritty plenty of gold we will try it as Soon as we can get over the Snow and if the mines are as good as they are reprsented [represented] we will mine it throu the Summer if not we will return to the City and try to get into Some Speculation I hardley know more what to wright for fear of a reputition of matter in my other letters which I think you probley will get

I hardley know wheather to Say we have had good bad or mediam luck but will give the amount of gold that John and I have on hand now and not in debt in Califonia the amount of gold Dust is Something near 8 lbs pure gold or Something near 23 carrets find our luck may be much better or much worse through the Summer we know not but good or bad we are bound to returne home at the appointed time. I doonot like Califonia it affords no charmes for me and especley in the absence of hir and onley hir that can make me happy Adeiu Dear Emma for the presant give my warmest affections to the children and all inquireing frends and curses to my enmeys   L C Bidamon

NB Nathen King is still with us and wishes you to tell his parenc [parents] that he is well and and trying to doo the best he can which is pretty fare

LCB

—Lewis Crum Bidamon, letter to Emma Smith Bidamon, 20 April 1850, Lewis C. Bidamon Papers, P12-2, f14, CofC Archives.

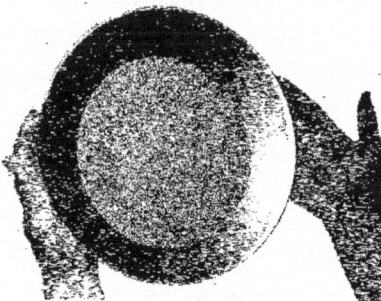

Biography *of* Julia Murdock Smith Dixon Middleton

Emma, David, and Julia Murdock Smith;
Detail of pencil sketch of the Homestead by David H. Smith

Julia Murdock Smith was born on 30 April 1831, the second born twin of John and Julia Clapp Murdock. The other twin was named Joseph. Their mother died as a result of the hard childbirth. Emma and Joseph Smith also lost a set of twins the same day and agreed to raise the Murdock twins as their own.

When Julia and Joseph were eleven months old, Joseph died as a result of exposure to the cold during the tarring and feathering of Joseph Smith, 24 March 1832. The family returned to Kirtland, where Joseph III joined the family in December 1832, and Frederick G. Williams arrived in June 1836. The Smiths resided in Kirtland until Julia was seven. As a result of turmoil within the church community at Kirtland, the family moved to Far West, Missouri. For the next several months, Julia and the Smith family enjoyed their new home and surroundings. Another son, Alexander Hale was born at Far West in June 1838. Joseph Smith and other church leaders were arrested on 31 October 1838 and soon the community of Far West was abandoned. During the winter of 1838-39, Emma Smith took her young family to Quincy, Illinois. On the way the weather was extremely cold. When they arrived at the Mississippi River, Emma took her two youngest sons, Frederick and Alexander in her arms. Julia and Joseph III held onto Emma's dress and together they all crossed the frozen river and safely reached the other side.

Emma and the children found refuge northeast of Quincy, Illinois, in the John Cleveland home. They remained there until Joseph escaped from Missouri authorities and rejoined the family in Quincy. In May 1839, the family moved to Commerce, Illinois, a town soon to be called Nauvoo. Emma taught Julia reading, sewing, and cooking. "As the new city of Nauvoo grew and matured, so did Julia. . . . Julia attended school for most of her years in Nauvoo." Julia's teacher, James Monroe, described Julia as a "bright pupil, particu-

Smith Homestead, Nauvoo, Illinois

larly in math, and somewhat of an independent thinker." Monroe once kept Julia and others after school. In a show of temper, Juila told the schoolmaster that he was "hard hearted" and that he "had no more heart than a hog."

During this same period Julia received art lessons and music lessons on a small portable organ.

When Julia was thirteen, her adopted father Joseph and uncle Hyrum were killed while incarcerated at Carthage, Illinois. Julia's biographer Reed Murdock observed, "The Nauvoo that Julia had known in the carefree days of her youth ceased to be." The family had to leave Nauvoo for a while for their own safety.

When they returned, Emma operated the Nauvoo Mansion

House as a hotel to provide a livelihood for Julia and her siblings. Julia's brother Joseph III observed that "the Mansion House became the center for social activities in Nauvoo;" and the young adults, Julia and Joseph, were thrown in the midst of it all.

In December 1847, Emma Smith married one of Nauvoo's new residents, Lewis Crum Bidamon, giving sixteen-year-old Julia a new stepfather. The marriage brought security as well as a degree of peace and tranquility to the Smith siblings.

During the winter and spring of 1849-50, a young itinerant named Elisha Dixon boarded at the Mansion House. During his

Julia at the portable melodian, hand tinted drawing by Sutclife Maudsley, 1842, courtesy LDS Church Library

stay due to an extended illness, Julia fell in love with the personable young man.

Julia Murdock Smith, was the first of the Smith children to marry. Julia and Elisha were married in early 1850 and left Nauvoo together. They lived for a time in Galveston, Texas. Elisha found work on a steamboat and was generally away from home. Julia's loneliness prompted several letters to Emma. In 1853, Elisha was killed in a steam boil-

Emma Smith Bidamon, ca. late 1870s

er explosion, and Julia returned home to be with Emma and the boys. During this time, Julia also corresponded with Joseph III who was away from home studying law.

In 1857, twenty-six-year-old Julia married John Middleton and moved to a small farm two miles south of Nauvoo. In a few years, John sold his farm and moved to St. Louis, Missouri. John seemed to fail at everything he attempted. In 1877, Julia left him and returned to Nauvoo. In addition, Julia was beginning to suffer from the effects of breast cancer. Once again she became part of Emma's and Lewis Bidamon's home.

After Emma's 1879 death, the James Moffatt family cared for Julia. Julia died in 1880 and was buried in the Nauvoo Catholic Cemetery.

—Based upon Reed Murdock, *John Murdock: His Life and His Legacy*, 269-72, 276, 297; Newell and Avery, *Mormon Enigma*, 54; Diary of James Monroe, Yale University; see *Enigma*, 214-15; 350, note 21; 272-73; Joseph Smith III, *Memoirs*, 50.

Composite pencil sketches of Nauvoo scenes, by David H. Smith

Correspondence *with*
Julia Murdock Smith
Dixon Middleton

Julia Murdock Smith, Daguerreotype, ca. 1855, Nauvoo, Illinois

Family Heirloom

JULIA DIXON, letter to Emma Bidamon:

Fremont House Galveston
March 25th 1852

My Dearest Mother

Your kind and affectionate letter was received with feealings of pleasure I cannot exspress pleasure in hearing from you and with Sorrow that we were So far Seperated from one another for It reminded me pain fully of It in reading your letter and in Seeing thos[e] Drawings of Davids God Bless his little Soul for remembering his absent Sister and tell him his Sister had a long Criing Spell over them and She Kissed them over and over again and (She will treasure them long as a Holey prise) as one of my favorite Songes goes I wish I could See him to night and Kiss him I often think of you all I can ashure you and Dream of you to[o] for you are never out of my thoughts my Dear Mother and I Some times immagin I can See you all as I left you the last time I Saw you the Boyes and Zeralda were in the North Room and you were in the front Door and Joseph was beside the Gate and So you all were the last time we Shook one another by the hand or that we imprinted the last Kiss on one anothers cheack and

I bid you adue for a time but may God in his mercy Grant It may not be for ever and I believe and trust It will not for every night I breath a prayer to him to Grant that we may all meet again in this World and he has promised that if we prayed in Sincerety of H[e]art we Should receive and in this promis I trust to See you and hope It will be before a while many more months have passed Mr Dixon has not made up his mind w[h]ether he will Stay here this Summer or not as we do not know how It will agree with us at present I am well I never was as healthy in my life before and I am as fat as a Bare [bear] So I think It will agree with me but I do not Know how It will Suit Mr Dixon he thinks he will Keep well but I am afraid not for already he has had a Billious attact but the Doc—Seams to think he will get along after he gets over this but you Know he is Subject to thos[e] attacts all this Winter he has been very healthey he weighed one Hundred and thurty until the warm we[a]ther came on and he has not felt so well Since he is now on the Steam Boat Magnolia gon[e] up Trinity River he has been gon[e] a week to Morrow and in another week they will be Back I am in hopes this trip will Cure him and I think <It will> for he wrote me from the mouth of the River that he was bet-

A steamboat like the Magnolia, Trinity River, Texas

ter and all the time was improving It is very healthey here now and they all Seam to think It will be all Summer I was talking to the Doc—a few dayes since about the Yellow Feaver he says It is not half as bad to cure as our Chills and Feaver and he Says that a person coming here if they have It they become Climatied [sic] and are more healthey afterwards So I do not dre[a]d It as much as I did. You wished me to tell you how It agreed with me I think much better here than at Home you would be ashtonish would you not if I told you I had Suffered with the heat to day but It is verily So It has been as hot here to day as It is at Home in June but we have one advantage here we always have a fine brease blowing from the gulf and at times It blows pretty hard we have here at times what they call Northers they come up in ten minets Sum times and they are awfull the first one we had after I came here frightened me very much It blowed for about three hours very hard It blowed the Dowar [door] down that devied [divided] the Galleryes here and It being in the Night I was frightened very much It Sometimes blowes So that It raises the tides and the water comes from the Gulf all over town and for dayes no one can get out onely on Drayes this makes It rather bad for you are liable to get your feet damp and make your Self Sick but this is a great place after all with all Its failings It is a beautiful place to See the Oreng [orange] and Lemmond [lemon] trees and the Spanish Dagger tree in bloom and all the most Beautifull flowers It is perfectly inchanting and the Figs Trees are full of leaves the Peach trees and the Chiney trees bloom Some time ago we have Peaches as larg[e] as a birds Egg now (Oh It is worth Seeing I Sincerly wish I could be Farrey [ferry] long enough to Sit you all down in the Suney South a few hours and I Know you would not want to go back again I wish you were all here to night It is a most lovely night the Moon is Shining in all her Splender you do not See Such nights at Home It is like Day light you could See to read without a candle Oh this is the land for me where we have warm dayes and beautiful cool Moon <lights> nights and where the breases that Fan your

Julia Murdock Smith Dixon, courtesy Dover Sindelar via Reed Murdock

brow come laden with perfumes from the Orenges and Lemmond Groves and the roar of the Gulf lulls you to Sleep and the Chirp of Gold Finch and Plover and Shrill Whisell of the Mawking Bird wakes you in the morning Oh is It not delightful I think so—we have Green Peas and Beans and Cellerey and Radishes now and that is Something more than you can say in the cold freezing North I think the Ladies are all out in there whites and Brozes [sic] and Jentes in White Pantealoons It looks So Strange I can hardly believe It is March but It is or els[e] the almanack lyes—You Sayed It was very cold when you wrote It was warm here then in fact I have not Seen eny cold we[a]ther here altho they make a great fuss about It they Say It was the hardest winter ever Known in Texas and if It was It was the only Cold we[a]ther they ever Saw I can tell them It was So ridiculas to See <how> asto[n]ished they were to See the Snow falling whi [why] does it fall in flakes sayes one as tho It would fall in Chuncks It made me laugh but I just inputed to there Ignorince and let them pass, you Say Grand Mother is coming to live with you I am glad to here It It will Seeam like old times once more wont It altho It will bee a great burthern to you how I wish I was there to help you you Say Uncle Arthur

Pencil sketch of dog, by David H. Smith

is goin to Calaforna I hope he will have better luck than Some men had who left here a few weeks ago to go there they went to the Ithsmous but could not cross there was ten thousand people waiting to cross and if they bought a ticket now they could not get of[f] before June so they concluded to come back & try It again next fall Your old friend Dave Birdsell is in Huston with his family or with what is left for he lost his Wife in Calaforna the repport is he has made a considerable money there he is goin back to the North Soon I understand—Mr Dixon Saw Mr Hannah a few weeks ago he is coming down here Soon he sayes and wants us to go Home with him and I exspect we will do So and Stay a few weekes he se[n]t his best respects to you about the Children you wanted to Know when Miss Hester and Mr Pease were goin to be Married I must assure you Short Never for I have no hopes that my wishes in this respect will ever be re-alised She is Surrounded by a great number of Devoted Admiriers but w[h]ether she will marry Soon or not is more than I can Say as for him I dou[b]t if he will be married ever—they boath Send ther love to you and the family—you must tell David I have only one Bird left the other two Dide tell him my Dog is doing well and is as much of a Pet as his Mistress is I am very Sorry to hear that Chloa is de[a]d but so goes the World and we cant help It—Ma I think the words of one of Moores Poems would Suite you—

Oh ever thus from child hoods hour
I have seen my fondest hopes decay
I never Nursed a tree or flower but
It was the first to faid [fade] and dy [dye]
I never nursed a Dear Gazell
to glad me with Its Dark bright ey[e] but
when It came to Know and love me well
It was Sure to dy [die]

I wish you would tell Zeralda to write to me and I want her to tell me all the news how they are over at Canton if Margret is Married yet and how they all get along I was very Much pained to hear of Mr Gleasons Death tell Mary I Morne with her in her great loss and Should like very Much to See her and time that heels every pain I Sincerley hope will be Mirciful to her give her my warm<est> love—tell Fred and Alex I was very much Delitited with there kind letters and I hope they will favor me with a great many Such I wrote to Fred Some four weeks ago and Mr Dixon wrote to Joseph and I am axiousley exspecting an answer from both of them you must all write often only think I have been from Home almost Six Months and have onley received two letters and this is the sixth we have writ[t]en So my books ar[e] posted and you can See if they are right I think they are I have some more portray [poetry] for you and It is my Setiments.

Oh Slow our Ship her foamy track
Against the wind was cleaving
Her trembling pennant. Still look'd back
To that Dare [dear] land twas leaving
So loath we part from all we love
From all the links that bind us
So turn our hearts as on we rove
To those we have left behind us.

And when in other Climes we meet
Some Isle ore rode enchanting
Where all looks flowery wild and Sweet
And not but love is wantiong
We think how great had been our bliss
If Heaven had but assigned us
To live and die in senis [scenes] like this
With Some we've left behind us

As travelers oft look back at Eve
When Southward darkly going
To gase upon that light they leave
Still point behind them glowing
So when the Close of pleasures day
To gloom hath near consigned us
We turn to catch one fading ray
Of joy that's left behind us

I wish when you write you would tell me all about the fuss at Sault Lake for I have never hurd about It I have written to cousin Marriah a long letter and have just written a long one to Mr Dixon's Sister so I have run a Shore for eny news to write I have not another Idea left and think you will have hard work to read this and keep your pasheants for It is so badly written but exscuse me this time I would like to hear from Mr Pressele [sic] when you write tell me how She is and now Dear Mother I think I will close Mr Dixon <sends> his love to you and the Children write Soon and remember me in your prayers at night for I do you I can ashure you Give my warmest love to the Children and all my friends Kiss David for me and tell him Sister Julia Sent It to him I wish he could write I know I would get Some long letters from him but good by for the present from your affectionate Daughter

Julia M Dixon

It is rather Croocked but never mind if you can read It I have written in a hury for the letter goes to Morrow on the Steamer and we only have a chance once a week of Sending our letters, So I must improve It.

(I have attended no parties here yet)

—Julia M. Dixon, letter to Emma Smith Bidamon, 25 March 1852, Lewis C. Bidamon Papers, P12-2, f17, CofC Archives.

David and Emma, detail from Nauvoo House painting by David H. Smith, ca. 1868, courtesy Lynn Smith Family

David Hyrum Smith, ca. 1870

JULIA M. MIDDLETON, letter to Emma Smith Bidamon:

St. Louis January 28, 1870
My Dear Mother

A happy New Years to one & all and many returns of the season. My New Years day was passed very quietly But thankfully to Almighty God for his many blessings to us in the last year that is gon. I first at eight oclock that morning went to mass where I prayed for all My friends not forgetting My Mother & Brothers. then I Came home & Built the Fires & got Breakfast for My self & Husband & to our surprise Robert joined us and in this meal which was very pleasant I assure you to have another face of The Dear old times at Table on that day. & we talked of the old times to[o] You may believe & of the Dear friends of Yore God Bless all of them[.] in the evening a few friends called on me, but as my Visiting Lists are small there was not many to call so passed the first of January 1870___[.] [lines in letter] Your letters of December 5 1869 January 9th 1870 have been on hand for a long time & every day I have promised myself I would answer them but Dear Mother I have not felt like writing to you untill we were more settled in our movements or were desided about staying here

but—I cannot wait any longer[.] John sayes Just tell all "You know my Husband has been sick for so long & also you Know he has done no Business for nearly three years now & as times are at present["]—It seems impossible for him to get any thing to do hear So we are obliged to sell our Home & give up all necessarys furniture & commence the world a new once more—Well this looks a little Hard but Dear Mother Trusting in our Good Lord I hope we shall come out all right yet. If John was fully restored to Health I would not care so much. but till he is I do not want to leave St. Louis, his Doctor sayes It would take a good Dr. to keep him from getting well now he is indeed well to what he has been but still there is a great deel to be done yet. his generiy [generally] Health is good. You would be surprized to see him so fair[.] his countainence has lost that dark sallow look he formerly had & his fresh fair & youthful looking now & his spirits are better more hopefull & Buoyant than he used to be but his leg is not yet well but It is decidedly better & improving Every day. the Doctor gives him every encouragement about that, he says It is almost miraculous the improvement already in his Leg & that it is getting well just as fast as It can—My Health is Splendid this winter not even a cold so far—Our Winter has been very mild but very sudden changes from warm to cold which has carried a great deal of sickness, very little snow since October, It is mild to night and feels like Rain. I was not a bit Huffy about the letter for I know My Dear Mother wrote & sent It as soon as she could & like her I feel glad she could do it in her time. Poor Dave I will write to him as soon as I can[.] tell him to write to me anyway, his letters are refreshing. God Bless him how glad he will be to get home again and what a fund of knowledge he will have gathered in his travils how I would like to hear him describe his impressions of the scenes he has passed through out in that Grand Country [mission to Utah and California] he seems delighted with the part he was in when he wrote me. It seems to agree with his Health in that climate—I hope he will come home stronger in Health than ever he was before—Dear Ma—I am so Thankfull you have such good health but do take care of yourself & not work so hard "Oh, I wish I could see you to night,["] but I can only see your picture with Daves little Bald Head resting on your arm as he used to look when I Sang him to Sleep, So many years ago, [see photograph on page 21.] what changes

Emma and David Hyrum Smith, ca. 1845

has come since then. It makes me feel Quite Old to tern from this picture and look at the one of him taken at the Lake And think of rocking that young man to sleep in my arms (I could not do it now)—I was a little surprised to hear about Joseph [Joseph III's marriage to Bertha Madison after the death of his first wife Emma Griswold, 25 March 1869], I hope he has done well however & may she prove a faithful wife to him & a good kind Mother to his Dear little girls is my sincere wish "poor Dear Emma [Emaline"] If she could have been spared to rase them but it was not to be Gods Holy Will be done It always brings the tears to my eyes to think of her & our Dear

Kind Fred I pray for them too, I can Still do this for them If no more in this world I received a letter from my Old Friend Semantha Moffitt last week I was glad to learn from It that her Husband is getting better health you know he has been sick a long time God grant he may get well he is a good man. She gave me little news no more than yourself—She seems to have none to write,—It must be dry times up there as well as here We have no news here Is it terrible dull As to your Capitol Joke I have heard it spoken as a not very unlikely thing to happen that Nauvoo would be selected as the point on account of its commanding view & view & fine location & then too It would be more central. St Louis will never get it and I think, or in fact any Large City, so dont Laugh Ma It might be so yet in your day— What a destiny It would be for poor Nauvoo would it not—perhaps you dont want it to come there like some of your citizens I have heard of before now—Now Dear Ma—I think the length of this will make amends for my delay wont it. Pleas write soon & direct to John Middleton St Louis not give the street for very likely we shall be out of this House before I could get an answer, John sends best love & kindest wishes to my Dear Mother Remember me

kindly to all my friends
Your Loving & affectionate child
Julia M. Middleton
I return Daves picture in this.

—Julia M. Middleton, letter to Emma Smith Bidamon, 28 January 1870, Huntington Library, Lewis Crum Bidamon Collection, #HM35743.

John Middleton, courtesy of Dr. Clarendon E. Van Norman Jr., facilitated by Rick Grunder

JULIA M. MIDDLETON, letter to Emma Smith Bidamon:

St. Louis January 19, 1872
My Dear Mother

And the Loved ones all at Home a happy greeting to One & all And may health Welth & prosperity crown the New Year with Its various gifts—I hope you had a right Merrie Christmas, for there was enough of you most asuredly to have a good time I think If all were well & I hope you were, I had a real pleasant time very Quiet but so happy the day was fine which was a great help to keep a person cheerful. "John & I heard five Masses that morning before Sun up. Our Church was beautiful. I wish you could have Seen It[."] After mass we came home had Quiet little breakfast then I got up what John calls one of my Elaborat Dinners & indeed I had enough for a good sized family—My Turkey lasted the ballence of the Year until I had enough Turkey—Our New Year was very Quietly passed & If I could keep from thinking It would have been as happy no doubt as was my Christmas but the recollection of the days that are gon would Intrude themselves upon me in Spite of all I could do & although kind good Friends were not wanting to

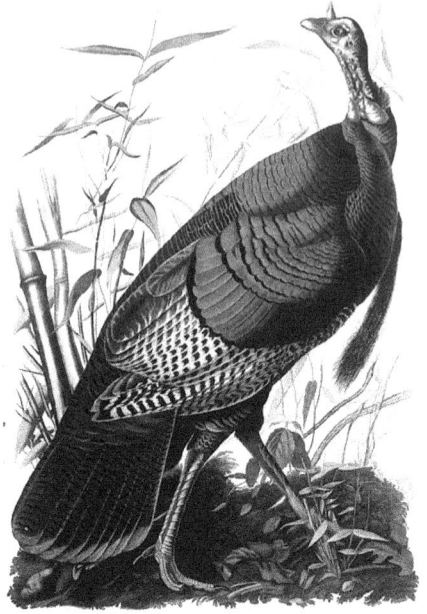

Wild turkey, by Audubon

wish me a happy New Year & Every good gift, Still I missed the Old familiar Voices & the kind familiar Faces from the Long go, When by going a Short Distance I could See My Own & My Husbands familys—Well the Memories of those days Serve to keep Green our feelings of Youth & Will last as long as Our Lives "I had three calls that day["] One was [by] my God Son a Bright Little fellow of Eight years old. So you see although We are living very Quietly I was not forgotten[.] You know New Years day is the Great day here for Gentlemen to call on their Lady friends & a right Good use they made of their privelig[e] this Year juding [judging] from the Great numbers [of] carriages I saw passing all day[.] "Even the Colord Gentry were out in full forse["] It was really amuseing to see them Apeing all the dignity & Pomposity of White people some of them too were Dressed in fine Style, but the most of them Walked in making there calls—I had a very pleasant Surprise Since the New Year commenced in receiving a good Picture of Zerelda [Lewis Bidamon's daughter] She Sent It by a Young Friend of Emmas that went home with them last Summer. It was right good of her to think of me after So many Years[.] poor Zerelda she always was good natured & kind to me. I will try & write to her Soon, as She asked me to when She called on me last August. Dear Mother I am very anxious to hear how your health is this Winter. I so often Dream of you & of being at home with you, but never in the new house, "by the by["] how does the New house sute[.] is It as comfortable as you anticipated

It would be—I have not any very [interesting] news, I believe to give you in regard to Ourselves. John is Still at Work & he keeps up first rate although his duties are very confining & consequently pretty hard for him still so far __ [illegible] as his part give perfect satisfaction but he is gon all day from early

Engraving of St. Louis, Missouri, ca. 1855, by Frederick Piercy

morn to late in the Evening the days I assure you Seem to me of unusual length & I Hale Sundays with joy for then he is home all day or nearly So. "John's leg gives him a good deal of trouble this winter.["] It is very large & last month he had to put on his [laced] stockings for pain. It swelled So We are having a long & very sever winter "Which no doubt you are already aware of["] but so far I have been out the worst days without any inconvenience Some how It Seems as though John nor I do not feel the cold as Severly as the most of persons here do "In doors our Room is to[o] comfortable to know how cold It is out["] Ma I have a stove that cant be Beat for it consumes less fewel & gives out more heat than any Stove I ever saw

"I often say I wish Ma had one like it.["] "Now Dear Ma do try & write me a few lines any way ["] & If you <cant> fill a Sheat of Paper make Dave write the rest & Say just what you want him to. John Joins in Love to you & the Major & Best Wishes to all   Your   Affectionate   Child Jute

[Along the side of letter] Love to all Alexs family Dave—& wife & Baby & to all my friends

—Julia M. Middleton, letter to Emma Bidamon, 19 January 1872, Lewis C. Bidamon Collection, #HM35745, Huntington Library (call). Reproduced by permission of Huntington Library, San Marino, California.

Cooking stove detail from Catharine E. Beecher, *The American Woman's Home: Or Principles of Domestic Science* (New York: J. B. Ford and Company, 1872), 74.

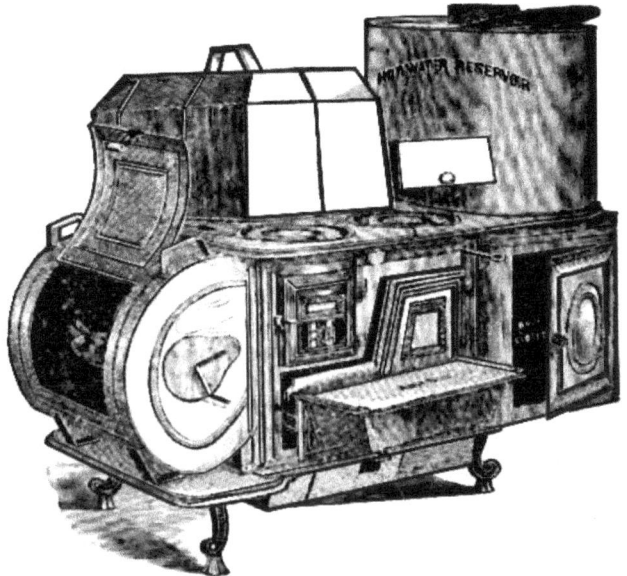

JULIA MIDDLETON, letter to Emma Bidamon:

St Louis Oct 4^{the} 1872

My Dear Mother

After waiting so long for an answer to my last I am again seated for the purpos of writing to that good kind Mother I long so much to see & not a day passes, she is not rememberd & prayed for by her absent Child, I wrote to you the 23 of July last & in the letter I enclosed a small gift of remembriance for my Mothers Birth Day but as I have not heard from you since I feel almost sure you could never have received It. I am so sorry to[o] for fear you will think I have neglected you & that too at a time you were suffering from your late accident but indeed I have felt very anxious about you & only that I heard from Dave that you had Quite recoverd from your Mishap I should have been Most Miserable, I hope I shall soon have the pleasure of reading one of your kind letters & of being assured that you are once more YourSelf able to do as you would wish without let or hindrence as far as your phisical & Bodily requirements are conserned "how did you stand the late Heated Term["?] It was fearful here for Ten days to two weeks there were from 16 to 27 Deaths a day from the Effect of the Heat John came Home one day very sick indeed & I had him to nurs<e> for nearly a Month & It is only within the last few Weeks he has felt like him Self in fact but now he can Eat & Sleep like a Chris[ti]an as he says him Self the nights during the very hot weather were worse than the day so that It was almost an impossibility for a person to rest, I never saw anything to Equal It & I very Much doubt If It could be Much hotter in the Tropicks I tell you the first Rain we had was hailed with joy for It brought Cool Nights & although It was only from one Extream to another, for It was chilly still It was most gratefully received

"Our City is pretty healthy now some alarm about Small Pox["] but nothing to feel very uneasy about I think so far our part of Town has been Quite free from the scourge, "We are just now in all the fixing & excitement consequent upon the holding of the Anual Fair of our City & bids fair to excell all the previous fairs so says modern Rumour["]—I went with my Husband & a young friend last Wednesday evening to hear a Lecture deliverd at the Sangerfest Hall here by the celebrated Fr Brook lately from Ireland & you form some Idea of what & Interesting speaker he must be when I tell you that for one Hour & Three Quarters he held spell Bound by his Eloquence 15,000 People the number in the Hall that night It was indeed a splendid sucess—Well Ma I must close for It is late, John joins me in kindest wishes & Love to you & the Major

Your Child as ever Juli[a]

—Julia Middleton, letter to Emma Bidamon, 4 October 1872, Emma Smith Bidamon Papers, LDS Church Library.

JULIA M. MIDDLETON, letter to Emma Smith Bidamon:

St. Louis Sept 8th 1873

My Dear Mother

Your most welcome letters of May June & August came safe to hand & It was to me a real Treat to get them & most eagerly I read them I assure you God Bless and preserve my Mother to write to me many more such kind good letters from now. It is such a Task for you to write, but Dear Ma It is such a great comfort to me to read one of your letters I have not the Heart to say don't write although It is selfish in me, but take your time to write them "Oh how much I wish to see you, but I don't expect to this year["] I hope to next If nothing happens to prevent my paying you a short visit—Your letter found us Quite well & doing as well as we can. "since I wrote you I had my old Galveston friend, Mrs. Andersen (Formerly Lizzie Levi) with me for a short visit ["]She came on Friday the 22 of August—& left Tuesday Evening the 26—I was so glad to see her again after Twenty Years time, I found her much changed of course but still she is the same warm Hearted friend as of yore "she is still a widow & in the Blackest of Black["] though her Husband is 9

David H. Smith Drawing

Drawing of a classically posed women which resembles Emma,
sketch by David H. Smith, ca. 1868

years Dead this month. She went south last May & It took her all this time to accomplish her object, namely the removal of the Body of her little Boy from Galveston. & the Building of a vault in another cemetary in New Orleans & the removal of her husband & her second son to It, & placing them with the one she took from Galveston, so they are at last all together & she has reserved a place in the vault for herself "poor child ["]she has been intent on doing this for years & has now accomplished It, My Heart aches for her she is so lonely her Father & Mother are still living but very feble she told me to tell my Mother she had been here & that she sent lots of Love to her I do wish I could have taken her up to see you I know you would have been pleased with her but She had been from her folks so long & they were so anxious for her return I could not keep her longer—I hope God will Bless her & hers for their kindness to me in the Darkest days I have ever known,—I am so glad you have heard from cousin Clara again, & I will write to her poor thing She has indeed had her own troubles you are mistaken Ma about this being the first letter she has wrote to you since she left Nauvoo she wrote to you, & me in 1859, & we both talked of answering her (I have the letter still) but—you remember

we were broke up sold out & came down here soon after & some way I never wrote to her but I will try & do better this time when you write to Aunt Wasson give her my warmest Love & best wishes I should be so glad to see her again I suppose she is with Carrie still I see the Rev. Mr DeWolfe is now at Decatur, Illinois or so the paper said some time ago & I took it to be Carries Husband was I right, I am looking for Dave's letter every day now & shall till I get It I am so glad to hear you are all so well & I pray you may all shall continue that same way & better too. If possible[.] give my Love to all, tell Lizzie I remember her kindness to me while up there & think of her often & her little family too I hope Master Fred is more careful about the axe now for I suppose while his Father is gon he is Man of the house—I can't think of any news to tell you so I guess I had better close this letter before I tire you out—

My Husband joins me in Kindest Love to our good Mother & the Major, from

Your Ever affectionate Daughter

—Julia M. Middleton, letter to Emma Smith Bidamon, 8 September 1873, Lewis C. Bidamon Collection, #HM35745, Huntington Library, San Marino, California.

Biography *of* Joseph Smith III

IN MARCH 1832, Joseph Smith Jr. returned to Ohio from Missouri, where he had gone to attend to church ventures. Avoiding the Hiram, Ohio, area, because of a recent encounter with angry residents, Joseph and Emma instead moved back to Kirtland. They took up residence with the Whitneys. Here Joseph and Emma's first child who grew to adulthood was born. Named after his father, Joseph Smith III was born 6 November 1832, above the kitchen at the rear of the Newel K. Whitney Store, at Kirtland, Geauga [now Lake] County, Ohio.

Kirtland began a period of spectacular growth, becoming quite crowded with gathering church members. By the time young Joseph was three, work was well underway on the erection of the Kirtland Temple, prominently positioned on the brow of the bluff overlooking Kirtland Flats and the Chagrin River.

In 1838, while Joseph III was still very young, his father was forced to flee Kirtland. Joseph Jr.

Joseph III leaning against middle column of the Newel K. Whitney Store building, Kirtland, Ohio, 1883

traveled west seeking refuge with the portion of the church living at Far West, Caldwell County,

Missouri. Joseph III remembered accompanying his mother, Emma Smith, as they made the journey from Kirtland, Ohio, to Missouri by wagon team. "The longer hills she climbed, at times walking in rain and mud and wind and storm."[1]

After a brief time of stability, the church was again forced to abandon its community at Far West. Some of Joseph III's earliest remembrances were of "being thrust" from the side of his father by the sword of an armed guard at Far West and making visits to his father in Liberty Jail with his mother. Joseph III observed,

> As pass the years of childhood to all, so passed the time to me; the removal to Illinois, the crossing on the ice, the reception at the farm of Mr. Cleveland, the return of my father from captivity, and the subsequent arrival at Commerce [Nauvoo], are like the unfinished pictures of memory to me. . . . Better times came, so that in 1840, and 41. . . . the town [of Nauvoo] was laid out, [and] buildings sprung up as if by magic. In 1842, the Mansion House was erected and our family moved in.

Joseph III was baptized a member of the church by his father in November 1843, "at the foot of Main street, Nauvoo." But

Brigham Young

this happy time passed altogether too quickly. Joseph further noted:

> At the death of my father, Joseph W. Coolidge was appointed administrator of the estate. Under his administration, besides the personal property allowed by law, there was allowed my mother $124 per year, for the support of her family. The private and personal correspondence of my father, many books and some other matters of a personal character were in his office in the care of Willard Richards, and others, clerks and officials. These were either retained by the administrator upon his own responsibility; or were refused to my mother's demand at the direction of the Twelve. . . .

Joseph Smith III, ca. 1873

Soon after the return to Nauvoo of Brigham Young, then president of the twelve, from the east, it became evident that there was to be a conflict between Sister Emma and Elder Young . . . . Sometime in the Summer of 1845, or possibly in the Fall, mother was made aware that she was an object of suspicion to the leading element of the Church; and that a watch was set over herself and her household. Persons visiting her house were watched and their footsteps dogged; some were turned away from her door, without being permitted to hold communication with the household; and upon one occasion a man, a friend, was assaulted, and but for his resolute defense of himself, would have suffered severely. At one time, word was sent her to vacate her home, and that if she remained in it after the expiration of three days it should be burned over her head.

For us, however, flight was out of the question; my mother . . . gathered her children unto her, and sitting down with them around her, explained to them the danger she and they were in, and charged them what to do in case the worst came; and after kneeling with them in prayer commending them to God, all lay down to sleep. The dreaded night passed,—and the old house still stands unharmed by fire.

The lines of supervision laid round my mother and her family by her self-constituted watchmen grew closer and more offensive. Her opinion in reference to the policy of the leading men began to be known; the word "apostate," was heard coupled with Sister Emma's name.

A trusted member of the church . . . waited upon mother to ascertain what her feelings were in reference to following the church west. She informed him that she thought she would not go. . . . The elder . . . finally stated to her that it had been decided to offer her an opportunity to go; and that if she refused, it was "decided to make her so poor that she would be glad to beg pardon of the Twelve and follow them."

In the spring of 1846, many members of the church withdrew from Nauvoo bound for the west,

and new citizens began coming in. After a short visit at Fulton City, Emma's family returned to Nauvoo and Emma became the proprietor of the Mansion House hotel. "In December 1847, Emma married Major Lewis C. Bidamon, a new citizen who had been active in the defense of the city and who had traded into the ownership of [a] considerable amount of the property offered for sale by the outgoing saints." At this time, Bidamon operated a small dry goods trade with a Mr. Hartwell of Philadelphia. Joseph III recalled,

> I clerked in his store for a part of the time till the next summer, when mother put for me a few hundred dollars into a mercantile venture with the Major's goods and placing them in the old brick store. . . . After my mother's marriage to Major Bidamon, our manner of life changed but little. We still continued to keep the hotel.

> In January of 1855, I went to Canton, Illinois, there to prosecute my study of the law in the office of Hon. William Kellogg, at that time an able and influential lawyer of Fulton County. I remained there the better part of a year, visiting home in the spring and being present at the death of Grandmother Smith in May. . . . I returned home in 1856, owing to the want of means to continue my

studies at Canton, and began farm life with my brother Frederick as my partner. . . . October 22d of this year I was married to Miss Emaline Griswold.

Joseph III experienced a memorable vision while reflecting upon his future and possible role within the Restoration. The experience directed him to have nothing to do with polygamy, but rather to oppose it. Soon after, in 1856, George A. Smith, Joseph III's first cousin once removed, and Erastus Snow visited him and encouraged him to join with Mormons of the West. Later, in 1856 he was visited by Samuel H. Gurley and Edmund C. Briggs, on behalf of the fledgling Reorganization. But

Erastus Snow

Joseph III avoided any commitment at that time.

In 1857, Joseph's brother Frederick G. W. married Alice Jones. The couple took up housekeeping at the Smith family farm. Meanwhile, Joseph and Emaline moved into the family homestead beside the Mississippi River. Also, during this period, Joseph served as one of the justices of the peace for Nauvoo Township.

Young Joseph had another visionary experience in 1859. By means of the Spirit, Joseph III was given to understand: "I have given them [the residue of the Saints reorganizing at Zarahemla, Wisconsin] my Spirit, and will continue to do so while they remain humble and faithful." Joseph III recalled, that in April 1860, "My mother and myself made the necessary preparation and started from Nauvoo to Amboy, on the 4th of April 1860." At this conference Joseph accepted the invitation to become president of this small group of his father's followers whom he would shape into the Reorganized Church.

In 1865, this commitment led to his removal to Plano, Illinois, from Nauvoo and his mother. At Plano, Joseph III assumed the editorship of the RLDS Church periodical, the *Herald*. Though distant from Nauvoo, Joseph III kept in touch with his mother through letters and family visits.

When Joseph III's wife Emaline died at Plano in 1869, Joseph married Bertha Madison in order to provide for his young family.

"The Old Homestead," pencil sketch by David H. Smith

The RLDS Church relocated its headquarters in 1881 and Smith family subsequently moved to Lamoni, Iowa. Smith built a commodious house, known as Liberty Hall, on the western edge of the city. Joseph's second wife Bertha died in 1896 as a result of an unfortunate horse and buggy accident.

Joseph married Ada Clark in 1898, and the family moved to Independence in 1906. Joseph died in Independence on 10 December 1914. Joseph III is buried in Mound Grove Cemetery, northwest of Independence, Missouri.

—Based on Edward W. Tullidge, *Life of Joseph the Prophet* (Plano, Illinois, 2nd ed., 1880), 746-74. Quotation referenced note 1 is from Vida E. Smith, "Biography of Patriarch Alexander H. Smith," *Journal of History* 4, no. 1 (January 1911): 4.

Joseph III and Emaline Griswold were married from 1856 to 1869 and lived in Nauvoo, Illinois.

Bertha Madison and Joseph III were married from 1869 to 1896 and lived in Plano, Illinois, and Lamoni, Iowa.

Ada Clark and Joseph III l were married from 1898 to 1914 and lived in Lamoni, Iowa.

Correspondence *with*
Joseph Smith III

Joseph Smith III, Daguerreotype, Emma Smith Bidamon image in lower right corner, ca. 1855, Nauvoo, Illinois

Family Heirloom

JOSEPH SMITH III, letter to Emma Smith Bidamon:

Canton, Illinois, June 15th, 1855.
Dear Mother:
    I write by return of "Express" in order that you may see that I am

all alive and well. Today I entered upon my duties as Clerk of the City Corporate of Canton. Well, we arrived safely I believe, and I expended upon the road $2.00 and coming from Virgil we had a passenger from whom we received $1. dollar so that our expences [sic] were the great sum of $1. but I do not know whether they will get off so well going home. You look for them tonight but they start tomorrow.

Mr. White has written to Mr. Bidamon in reference to the Clark matter and sent a receipt, which provided he can get no more than the $75, he is to give to Clark, but if he can get more he is to insert the amount he can get in the receipt.

I am studying hard as I can, and will try hard to acquire the mysteries of the Law. The people send their respects to all. My picture will come after awhile when the frames come here from N. York they are not here so they can not send them over, but the pictures and tickets they bring with them. Jute and Alex will tell all the news so I will say goodbye.

My love to all, Jos. Smith

—Joseph Smith III, letter to Emma Smith Bidamon, 15 June 1855, Joseph Smith III Papers, P15, f1, CofC Archives.

EMMA SMITH Bidamon, letter to Joseph Smith III:

Sabbath evening
August 19, 1866

Joseph Dear

How often I have been made deeply sensable that my pilgrimage has been an arduous one and God only knows how often my heart has allmost sunk when I have reflected how much more arduous and trying your [work] was to be I have often thought that I know as well as any other person just how St. Paul felt when he said, If only in this life we have hope, we are of all men the most miserable.

Now you must not let those

Joseph Smith III, ca. 1866

not make such a hasty promise, if you have trouble and are weary or vexed with the wickedness of them that ought to know and do better why should you not next to God tell your Mother so that being the first complaint when you are troubled again give me the Second complaint and let [it] be a relief to your burthened mind. I would indeed like to help you bear all of your vexations.

Monday afternoon. I am very glad that Emma is better I hope that God will be merciful to her. Now as to Cousin Simmons story I know nothing about it, I only remember Julias telling about seeing Harmon in Texas it may be all true and it may not be, let it be which ever it may be I do not see the object of telling the tale to you on such short acquaintance. You ask who preached Mr. Smiths funeral sermon. It was Mr. Waldenmeyer, his text was a part of what St. Paul Said, the words were, I have finished my course. he gave us a very good account of Pauls life and labors while he lived but did not tell any thing about his fighting the good fight, or of keeping the faith, nor any thing about the reward that awaited him but just left poor St. Paul to Say he had finished his c[o]urse, to me it was rather dry browse, but to others it must have been better as you will see in the Nauvoo Herald, I will send it. I am

LDSes trouble you too much if they are determined to do evil they will do it and such as are anxiously willing to make you trouble are not worth laboring very hard to save from the dogs.

You may know that you are not the first one that has been misunderstood or misapplied nor misquoted and misrepresented in every way and in every conceiveable shape, neither is it certain that you will be the last one, if you bear affliction well the evil one will pehaps light up a little on you and go and vex someone else for a while.

Now Joseph I want you to take back those four or five words (it shall be the last[)]. I can pardon you for complaining, but you must sorry you have forgot what cherries are, I hope you will not forget the grapes if I could I would send you some just to keep you in remember-ance of them we are having some very nice and ripe but not a very great amount of them yet.

Pa Bidamon was gone to Can-ton eleven days, his trip improved his health and general condition so much that he quite insisted that I should fix up and go right off up to Plano, he was very confident that he and Aunt Elsie could take care of things as well as she and I had done without him I[t] was very kind in him and quite a temtation to me, for dearly indeed I would like to come up there and see you

Emaline Griswold Smith,
wife of Joseph Smith III

all and especially them children that I have not seen for so long a time. If I could leave every thing else I could not leave Lizie and the chil-dren Lizie's health and condition is such that I dare not go so far from her I must confess it is a little trying to my natural inclination & to let concience and a Sence of duty de-prive me of that much desired priv-aldge, but I must take care of Aex family faithfully as I can while he is gone, and especially as long as Lizie is in the helpless condition she is in now. If brother Rodgers can help her I wished he would She has had nothing only what Alex sent back to her yet, and that has only supplied some nessesary clothing. She has flower enough to last till spring and perhaps till harvest and the milk of her cow and the rest she gets at the table with me She has not got coal enough for winter.

I was told yesterday that Sister Anderson is in need of help imedi-ately but I do not know how true it is I think it will be well for to acer-tain. [The rest of the letter is miss-ing.]

—Emma Smith Bidamon, letter to Joseph Smith III, 19 August 1866, Emma Smith Papers, P4, f31, CofC Archives.

EMMA SMITH Bidamon to Joseph Smith III:

August <Oct> 11th 1866

Joseph

yours of Sept 25 was received a long time ago, but not answered un-till [sic] now. As to your poetical ef-fusion I shall keep <it> safe if I can. I think it will be something to look at when we all get together again. The Lizie Fisher that died was the stone keepers oldest daughter, a very good girl, and it is a severe loss to her parents.

Now Joseph as for David I am as much at a loss what advice to give as you can possibly be, and I shall submit the matter to yourself and him. Your letter speaks of his being a teacher. I would ask (of what) of music, or painting or both. I would like to have him know something about legal lore as you call it, if he could obtain it with out too much sacrafice of other things I believe a little knowledge of common law helps a man sometimes to keep out of the limbos. I know very well that if your Father had been a lit-tle acquainted with the laws of our country he might have avoided a great deal of trouble. And yet I have a horror of one of my children be-ing entirely dependant upon being a lawier for living. but let him and you decide as best you can and then leave it to his steady and faithful percirverance and the kind blessings of our heavenly father and I think it will all be right in the end

Oct 2nd was received last week and I felt very gratefull for the in-formation concerning Davids good condition.

As for Alexanders doing much with the Smiths at Salt Lake is a doub[t]ful question with me. I think it right for him to go and dis-charge his duty to them and leave them without excuse I look upon their case as a hard one I believe God is able to do all that is for his glory and the good of those that

Cousin John Smith, Hyrum's son, of Utah

truly serve him, and may be that God may consider them in their ignorance and convict and convert them and cleanse them from their abominations and make them fit for more decent Society. I hope he will. that is those that was taken there when too young to know any better, they may come and Stand with you. but you can never stand with them there as they are now. I pitty your Society there if that Mrs. Sharon is any more of a carnally m[n]atural being than we have had her hanging on to the verge of the church, but we are in hopes that one or two is about sliping off We have had an advent into our place within the last two weeks of the Bishops that is the old man and his wife Amos and his wife and two children a Mr Lutes and his wife, a Sister of Mother Bishop, Fred and his wife are on their way in the Photo Car and when they get here I shall try and get my shaddow taken to send to you as there is now no other chance as Miller has done nothing in the business all this sumer nor never will, in fact he is geting to be allmost a nuisance too lazy to do anything.

The idea I wished to convey with regard to Pleasant Chat was that it was so interesting to me that each number left one in allmost breathless anxiety for the next one

There is no difference in the in-formation in Alex letters to us and that to you.

I donot know how it happened that your pig and ours should have been so much alike, in their conclusions all the difference was ours prefered being buried by the river, but we have no one in its place.

Our old neighbour Mr. Presel [?] stayed here last night having lately returned home from serving his country five year he looks fat and hearty and enquired very particularly about you and Alex and David and then about Frederick as he had never heard of his death. It is time to get supper so I must bid you good bye and may Heavens blessing be with you is the prayer of Your Mother   Emma Bidamon

—Emma Smith Bidamon, letter to Joseph Smith III, 11 October 1866, Emma Smith Papers, P4, f32, CofC Archives.

Emma at Nauvoo, Illinois, around 1866.
Image digitally edited by Marvin Crozier

EMMA SMITH Bidamon, letter to Joseph Smith III:

Oct 22nd 1866

Well Joseph it appears to be a fact that the weather there and the weather here is very nearly, or quite exactly the same but I think it has a different effect upon me from what it has on you, for I am very certain I did not feel very poetical last Monday. I learned today that our Nauvoo Herald has subsided. I am not much disappointed, tho I thought perhaps it might posibly exist untill after the Nov election, but it is gone.

I forgot in my last letter to tell you that Sister Revel is here. She has been here a little over two weeks, her soninlaw was sick some time before she left St Louis. She received a letter about a week ago that he was dead and she is expecting Brother Revel and the widow and family up this week, so the old folks have some thing to do to take care of that family here in this place. There has been a company of civil engineres encamped just across the river for about two week[s], engaged in making a preliminary survey for a Ship Canal, but we can learn but very little about the buisnes from them.

Gen Harding has been here and made a great speech, and left us very great assurances that the goverment would build that Canal, on this side of the river the good old General was uncomonly sociable and friendly, and appeared to be perfectly confident that Nauvoo is to be a great place yet. Gen Fonda was here with Gen Harding, and he is the same quiet unasuming man that he was before he became a Gen. I think he is more sociable than he used to be.

Alex was well on the [4th] of Oct was in the town or city of Austin, and if he has had good luck, and no bad luck he must be in California by this time. O how I hope he will get through safe. I very well know he has had some hard times.

We are having six boarders now, they are masons from Fort Madison and are building an addition to the house that Morrel formerly owned.

There is a man stoping here that says he is a brother of M M Tilton and I think he is, he looks very much like him. Mrs. Bishop tells me they do not now look for Fred till spring so I can not get those Photos. Our meetings are rather poorly attended we have some members that are not much account. the outsiders have left off attending. I think some of them are a little like myself, they miss my boys. Sister Alston died last week Mr Walters buried one of his little boys yesterday, the young-

RLDS meetings were held in
the Red Brick Store, during the 1860s.

est but one, that one is about four
weeks old.

There was a car run off the track
just this side of Nashvill a few days
ago one man killed instantly and
thirty hurt fifteen badly, some have
died of the injuries November 11
Two weeks ago this evening I commenced this letter maybe I shall
finish it this night and may be not
Brother Revels folks are all here and
are settled in their old place.

And now Joseph I must tell you
about a certain advent we had here
one week ago last Tuesday night
in the shape of two females an-
nouncing themselves as coming
from Plano direct from brother
Josephs and the moment they said
Plano I knew they were your two
[vex]turals [vexatious women] you

mentioned some time ago they did
not throw themselves on the church
exactly, but came down on us in the
Mansion for a home. I gave them to
understand the first evening that it
was not convenient or even possible
for me to give them implyment or
a home that they must seek some
other place but they appeared not
to think as I did about the matter
and stayed three days and of course
I lived and let live and did not comit
any very outbreaking sin, but if they
had not left after being told to every
day I believe I should have commit-
ed some [end of document]

—Emma Smith Bidamon, letter
to Joseph Smith III, 22 October
1866, Emma Smith Papers, P4,
f33, (fragment), CofC Archives.

Joseph Smith III, 1864

Emma Smith Bidamon

EMMA SMITH Bidamon letter to Joseph Smith III:

Nauvoo [no month] 30 67

Well Joseph

All is well here at this time, and if there is no unforeseen, unthought of, undesirable, unlucky, unfortunate or any other, of the disagreable, uns, transpires here to obstruct my progress I shall get up about three oclock on this Thursday morning, and at four I shall take a brief leave of absence of home and go up to the ferry. brother Gifford says he will put me over the river at any time if it is at midnight, even if it should blow, and rain as bad as it did eight year ago, when he and dear Fred took you and I over. Well, bless Brother James, I think I shall have plenty of time to get to Hamlinton by eight.

My prospects are unusally good at present, so look for me when you see me coming.

The weather is, and has been beautiful now for several days.

Rose has been having a series of fits, but today she appears all right again. I am glad that it is over before I leave home. She will not be likely to have any more before I come home again. She is very much broke, but not as dificult to get along with as she used to be.

May the spirit of God be with us all. Emma Bidamon

—Emma Smith Bidamon, letter to Joseph Smith III, Nauvoo, 30 [no month] 1867, Emma Smith Papers, P4, f34, CofC Archives.

EMMA SMITH Bidamon, letter to Joseph Smith III:

Nauvoo Jan 20 1867

Dear Joseph

I am highly gratified to find my house quiet, and I think it will be so all day for it blows and snows right from the country where you live, we have had but a few days of very severe cold weather so far this winter the river has not been closed here yet, but if it keeps on as it is doing now it will be before long

I am very thankfull that you are getting along so well with the Manuscrips, and have truely faithful companions to help you. God bless them with the light of his spirit. It is true that not every L.D.S. could be trusted, to coppy them, and I did not trust many of them with the reading of them and I am of the opinion that if I had have trusted all that wished for that privaledge [sic] You would not have them in your posesion now.

Tell Brother Rogers that Lizzie and her little ones are in good health at presant, and have been well provided for so far the mony he sent her is all she has had from the church, and A[l]ex has sent her some mony and will send her more as soon as he gets her answer of the receipt of what he has sent her, she has no mony [sic] now and will have to be helped to a little before long if Al[e]x does not send her some. The matter of your taxes had been under consideration by Pa Bidamon and Pa Austin two days before I received your letter containing the fifteen dollars just as you advised us to do in your letter so Pa Bidamon and myself keeps still about the mony received and will let Pa Austin do what he can. if he makes out anything well if not we will see that the taxes are paid, tho our texes are very high this year, yours is sixteen dollars You understand Pa Austin can do nothing himself towards paying any thing but thinks he can get the rent of the ice house in advance and then try the church for the balance, if he succeds Pa Bidamon wants to know if he may apply the fifteen dollars on that school mony debt as he has got the Squire to wait till the first of April before he issues anexecution. The little paper with my name on it that is on the Tribune say 23 June 67. Now let Emma write as often as she likes to, it will do her some little good, and it certainly does me a great good. I do not know that any one really envies me the satisfaction I enjoy in receiving so many such kind good letters, but one thing I do know that there is a great many parents that would be proud if not thankfull if their children, and grandchildren had the affection and talent to write to them as mine have does to me, that little new year letter that Emma sent me is a gem, I shall preserve it as long as I live if I can I can read your letter very well if Carrie and Zaida did help to write it, and the ideas are very well connected notwithstanding the altercation between brothers Shippy and Robinson.

I sent the big bible as you directed, hoping and praying that it may accomplish its mission and be as much comfort and consolation to you as it has been to me, I have kept it lying on my little table ever since David went away, and now I have got the old bible that Judge Young gave to your Father, which you will reccolect was printed in 1650[.]

Now Joseph pardon me for forgetng [forgetting] to send you the directions for making that salve before this. I should have made some and sent it with the old bible but I was not well enough to do it then and I expected you would not like to wait any longer for the book than could be helped, so I will tell you now how I make the salve, Of sweet elder bark a good large handful after it is scraped, and as much gymson leaves and buds if they are green and tender enough to be pounded up fine, put them in a skillet or small kettle, and cover them with water and boil

them about twenty minutes, then take it of[f] and when cool enough strain the liquor through a cloth that is strong enough wringing so as to get all out of the dregs that can be got, then put the liquor back in to the kettle and boil it about half away, then put half a pound of mutton tallow, half a pound of bees wax and let it simmer nearly down to a fry, then take it off and put one ounce of camphor gum into it and stir it keeping it warm till the gum is all disolved try it on a rag and if too soft put a little more wax if too hard a little tallow, if you want a salve that will drane take a part of what is made and disolve a small piece of rosin in it Now if you did not save any gymson last fall you can make it with the elder alone.

The first camphorated salve I ever made, was just mutton tallow and bees wax and camphor alone and it was then thought to be an excelent

Sketch of Emma Smith by David Hyrum Smith, ca. 1860s.

article if you have not the gymson and elder let me know it and I will send you the salve ready made All I can do for the committee and brothers Blair and Shippy to recompence them for their kind rememberance of me is to pray that our Heavenly Father will bless them both temporally and spiritually and that the records which I was the then humble instrument in saving may be in their hand a perfect shield to parrie off all the malignant thrusts of the enemies of the truth you say news to me. Why: I have none I do not blieve I have any of any kind, not even lies, I believe the tatlers have all got tired of telling me any thing I cannot tell why unless it is because they have to tell somebody else their tales before they can get them into circulation

It may be interesting to you that Mr. Waldenmyer and M M Morrell has gone to Springfield to get a charter for Our railroad

It is reported that there is a convention called to meet at St. Louis the first of Feb to take into consideration the construction of the Canal round the rapids, three delegates from Nauvoo ten from Warsaw ten from Keokuk, etc etc. I have not seen the notice, but understand it is in the St. Louis Democrat this sheet is longer than a gnats wing but not large enough to take all I would like to send

God keep my dear children all safe till I can see them all again.

Your mother Emma Bidamon

[upside down top of page 3] Now Joseph fetch Carrie and Zaida down here in the spring and I will turn out Fredy and Vida to mach [sic] them in turning up matters and things while any one is writing

—Emma Smith Bidamon, letter to Joseph Smith III, 20 January 1867, Emma Smith Papers, P4, f35, CofC Archives.

EMMA SMITH Bidamon, letter to Joseph Smith III:

Nauvoo Feb 2 1866 [1867] Dear Joseph It is now eight oclock and <I> have just got Seated to answer your two last letters. And I feel very much like objecting to your too close application to your pen. I do not want you to torture your bra<i>ns too much now, for if you live to be as old as I am <and I believe you> will you will find plenty of use for them, and will want them in a good healthy and active State. So now take care of those brains and do not abuse them, for I think they are composed of better material then some others in this world.

I looked in the Herald and found there <the> balance of your note. it is too good for me. I feel very unworthy of So many good and pressious tokens of respect, and allmost veneration, from you, my Son, and your faithful and much respected brethren in the work of preparing the New Translation, God bless you and them, with the light of his holy Spirit. Those lines in the Heral[d] caused me to retrospect those years of mine portrayed in them and I find not one thing in them that I done, which was not just Simply my duty to do, and that too without Stoping to anticipate any future reward, so that the happines I now am enjoy-

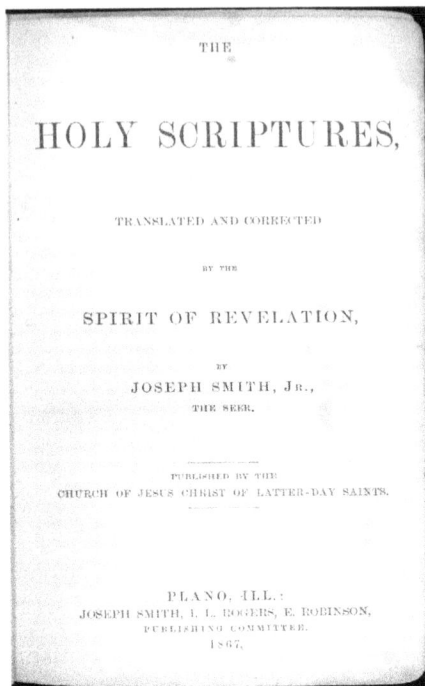

Joseph Smith Jr.'s translation of the Holy Scriptures, published by the RLDS Church, 1867

ing is all new and unexpected I am indeed truely thankfull that <the> translation is what the good and cincerely honest have looked for but there are Some that are So blinded with their own Self conceit that they will cavil tho the word may be So plain that a fool can understand.

I hope that Wm E McLellen will unearth his long burried telents, and get them into circulation before it is everlastingly too late for his own good as well as for the benefit of others, for he is certainly a talented man. I received a letter last evening

Joseph Smith III, 1869

I hardly think that there will <be> much difficulty to Settle here in the Spring. You ask how we prosper in all and every way. Well I Suppose you mean here at the old Mansion. Pa Bidamon is well all except his right Shoulder, that has the rheumatics badly. Aunt Elsie is well and as well contented as I ever knew her to be. and She begins to think of getting a home of her own if She can get a good chance. Lizzie and the children are well and get along finely She received a letter from Bishop Rogers last evening with thirty dollars in it which made her feel quite light hearted this morn Adison Crouch is as good a boy as could be expected if you look at his Mother. it is late and I must Stop till tomorrow

Feb 3rd Well it is today now and it is a warm and pleasant day and I must now tell you about myself as the last one in the house. I never lived a winter with So little hard work to do as I have So far this winter and we have a plenty of meat, and potatoes and crout in abundance, flour, and corn meal, milk, and butter of our own make, apples, and apple butter, marmalade and jellies and dried cherries, and hominy, and beans dried Swett corn, and—and, so forth and I am blessed <with> a good appetite. and eat more and Sleep more than I ever did before,

from Emma J which tells <of> a good many things that are going on there at your home in such a natural way that I can allmost See them, but She forgot to put those Samples of their dresses in the letter, So She will have to write me another, it also gives good evidence of her improvement Pa Astin [Austin] brought me your tax receipt and wished me to write to you as it was Such hard work for him to write. John Kendall paid the taxes on the wood land and gave the receipt to Brother Redfield The fifteen dollars goes on the Sonora case

Sketch of double cornucopia, by David H. Smith

one trouble I have, that is I often go to bed without being either tired or Sleepy and find it hard to rest when not weary, and Sleep without being Sleepy. but I think I Shall be in good condition when the Spring comes to work at what ever comes to hand I hope I Shall when you and your family comes on that promised visit. I cannot think of any thing at presant concerning the New Translation that would be interesting to the Committee. if there is any thing, or any question you or they have on your minds just let me have it, as I know of nothing that I am not willing to tell you about that matter.

I have not had my Negative taken yet. and I do not know but that I might as well look for the Car of Well of Jugernot as look for Fred Bishops car but Amos Bishop has rented Millers old concerns and is

expected to go at the buisness next month and if he does I shall try to get my No [negative] taken.

Pa Bidamon received a letter from Col Thornton a few days ago in which he gives Some evidence of an encouraging nature that there is Something a going to be done about our old rail road. The Col said he was coming down as Soon as he could. So we are expecting him. now it has become pleasant weather.

Alex['s] taxes on the farm are not paid yet. John A went on yesterday to See the Collector and had the money to pay but Temple could not give a receipt without the deed. it appears the land you Sold to Lenhart and Fredericks past and Alex is not divided on the town books and it is all assessed to gether. and it is rather doubtful whether John will be able to get it Straight It is truely generous and noble in you to Sympathise in the afflictions of Aunt Nancy, and Uncle Christian If there is any thing in this world that I am, or ever was proud of it is the honor and integrity of my children but I dare not allow myself to be proud, as I believe that pride is one of the Sins So often reproved in the good book. So I am enjoying the better Spirit, and that is to be truly and cincerely thankfull and in humility give God the glory, not trying to take any of it to my Self for it is him that has led my children in the better way. it is true that I Sometimes feel lonely in the absence of my own dear ones. but then I have no horrid fears of their ever being guilty of what we must believe John Bidamon is. No one knows the Solid heartfelt pleasure I take in comparing my Sons with others and then, too that [t]hey had fathers of their own to guard them. Pa Bidamon would like to know in what way Judge Kellog has played out. Pa Austins family are now talking of leaving here in the Spring, and if the Spirit that has ruled that house ever Since the boys came home is to remain predominant among them I think the Sooner they go the better for the church here. this I say to you, but would not to any <one> else remember me in love to Emma and the children.

God bless you all is the prayer of your mother Emma Bidamon

Will Stephenson and wife was here yesterday and requested me to give their love and respects to you and David

—Emma Smith Bidamon, letter to Joseph Smith III, 2 February 1866 [sic, 1867], Emma Smith Papers, P4, f36, CofC Archives.

Pencil and tinted sketch of a candle, by David H. Smith

EMMA SMITH Bidamon, letter to Joseph Smith III:

Nauvoo Feb 10th 1867

Ever dear Joseph

Yours of the 2nd came in fridays mail you tell us of a snow storm in your place that day but we had none here. it was a bright day untill nearly night when it clouded up but did not storm till friday then we had a real snow squall right from the north and it has been as cold as greenland untill this afternoon and now it is geting more plasent. My heart is made glad by your report of your progress in the translation as you know something of my fears with regard to its publication, on account of what your Father said about the unfinished condition of the work. Now Joseph I am afraid you are giving me more credit for the past I have acted in the matter than I realy deserve. I sent the old bible to you, but you have not told me that you have got it yet, please let me know if you have next time you write.

I received another letter from John Smith and in the same envelop one for Julia with his photo in Julia's requesting hers in return. I do not know what has come over him to be so mindful of us just now.

I suppose you are aware that Pa Austins folks talk about going away

1828 Phinney Bible, used by Joseph Smith to mark biblical revisions

in the spring and there is some that begin to talk about the premises brother Bradley from the country has applied to John Kendall to speak for the chance to rent them for his family as he is talking of going west to look for a better country to live in. Now I cannot give any advise because I have not been asked for any but I should like to have you see the place before you rent it.

I like the Herald and the talk on tithing I think is what the church has needed very much as I do not believe that one half of them knew what it meant. Ab[o]ut the book of Enoch I have not sense enough to understand it, or what it is for I know I am very stupid about some things and perhaps I am about that.

I hope you feel better by this time as I am sure it would be bad for you to be sick.

Amos Bishop does not go into the picture gallery but there has been a gentleman boarding here a few days who says he is going to work as soon as he gets his things here. He is now gone to Keokuk after them so if he does not fail I may yet have a chance to get some photos taken.

All the folks are well. tell Emma I shall answer her letter before many days remember me to your wife tell her I would like another letter from her very much

God bless you all good bye Your Mother Emma Bidamon

—Emma Smith Bidamon, letter to Joseph Smith III, 10 February 1867, Emma Smith Papers, P4, f37, CofC Archives.

EMMA SMITH Bidamon, letter to Joseph Smith III:

Nauvoo Dec 2 1867

My own dear Joseph

It has been a long time since I have written to you or any one else. I think I have only written two letters to you and one to David and only one to Alex since last March but it has not been because I have ever forgot to write neither has it been because I did not want to write but it has been a combination of all things about the house which has kept me so muddled that I could not write in daylight and my old spectacles has been broke and I could not see to write by lamp light, but I have just got a new pair today and I am now trying them. We have had a good many boarders ever since you were here untill last week. Mr. Napier covered up his quarry and will leave tomorrow then we shall have but one steady boarder and that is the school teacher his name is Tucker not old [Lew] Tucker but Charley Tucker and he is allways in season to his meals I would like to tell you all about what is and what has been going on here since you was here but I cannot in this letter and I have not yet had time to look over all the letters you have sent to me that remain unanswered but I think I shall before long and I am determined to write at least one letter to your four and I look for one every week just as much as tho I answered all yours seperatly and individually. I was very anxious to see you on your return from Conference, as I had so little chance to see and talk with you when you was here that it allmost seemes as tho I had not seen you for an age. I wanted you should see the old homestead as it was left as I did not like to write the whole truth but I expect John Kendall has written all about it before this.

I would like to know something about that grave yard fence, why the old man left it just as it was when you was here, and what you think about trying to have it put up the coming spring I have allways felt sad about the neglected condition of that place and as I do not expect ever to be able to build me a house to live in I would like to fix a place to be put away in when I have done all my work on the earth 3rd Joseph I should like if you are willing to extend that fence so as to enclose the graves of your two little brothers. I have got twenty five dollars that no one has any right to but myself, ten I got of Governor Stones wife for that picture that Mrs Slatham left here and fifteen a Sister Adams in California sent to me. no one here knows any thing of the fifteen except Lizzie and I feel anxious to apply that money on that grave yard, after I have done that I think I can ask our Smith relatives to help mark Fathers and Mothers graves if no more. Now as it regards the MS of the new translation if you wish to keep them you may do so, but if not I would like to have them. I have often thought the reason why our house did not burn down when it has been so often on fire was be-

cause of them, and I still feel there is a sacredness attached to them.

The summer and fall has been very dry, we have had no cold weather nor any storm of any kind untill the 27 of last month, then we had two days of biting cold, yesterday and today has been pleasant. The grape crop was only about one third of a good crop our South vinyard done the best of any about here except Mr Beverstoffs the west vinyard did not do so well. I think we had some of the largest clusters and the largest berys on them that I ever saw, and we used them freely. We eat all we wanted and made pies by the section, caned a few made some jelly, put up a box to be opened when you come from Conference, put up another box to keep till Alex come home sold one or two hundred and then made over three hundred gallons of wine and a cask of vinegar. Pa Bidamon would not have made any wine if he could have sold the grapes as he did last year but he could only get from five to seven cents a pound

I would like to tell you some thing about the church here if I had any thing good to tell, but I have not so I will only say that it is in a very low condition

Joseph I do not know but you have been informed that brother Redfields folks are gone and brother Cutlers family also and I do not know but it is the best thing they could do, yet I believe they might have done better. Mor[e] I cannot tell you any thing about the new faction that is being got up by Shaw, Lambert, Miller and Cuerden for I do not know but a presious little about it myself, but it seems by what I have heard about them that they are a going to make their folly manifest to all that has a particle of desernment.

I have received three letters from Julia since I have written to her and I cannot remember her numbers and I have lost that little slip of paper I sent to you to get desiphered and I wish you would send her figures in your next letter. I have not had but two short letters from David since he went to Wisconsin

We are all well today and this evening and it is nine oclock.

So Carry Griswold is married. well there has been been a number married round about here but the most redicolous of all was when Eugene Loomis was married to old Sall Grates, and now poor blue genes [nickname] is under bonds to appear before the court next term for stealing a cow and Fritz Fetter has got mixed up in the matter by some means or other and was arrested last Sunday night and is now in jail because he had no friend to go his security, poor fellow I am truely

sory for him. I infer from your letter that Aunt Elsie showed some of her venom up there as well as she did here where has she gone. I some times all most fear she will come this way again but hope she never will. Tell Emma and the children I have not forgotten them by a thousand times. So good night to you all God bless my dear children

Your Mother Emma Bidamon

Joseph when I come to look at my writing by daylight I can hardly read it myself.

—Emma Smith Bidamon, letter, to Joseph Smith III, 2 December 1867, Emma Smith Papers, P4, f39, CofC Archives.

EMMA SMITH Bidamon, letter to Joseph Smith III:

Nauvoo August 1 [ca. 1868-69]
Dear Joseph

I have a splendid pile of letters before me from you, all of which remain unanswered and <all> of which I would like to answer individually but fear I can not do it. I have been having a good deal of work to do for the last two months, and have no help except that girl that Lizzie could not keep, well I do not blame Lizzie for not keeping her she is a pretty hard case, but I think she is groing better she works much better than she did when she first came to live with me, so I think I shall get along better. Pa Bidamon has worked very hard this summer and he begins to think he can not do so another year, but I believe our hardest work is over for this summer as we shall <have> but very few grapes and perhaps none at all this fall, so he will not have the trouble of working them up. We have had such rains that every thing has been gloomy, but yet I do not feel like being disheartened neither do I feel like giving up work yet. I do not know what may happen to put a stop to our taking care of ourselves till Alex and David shall have accomplished there mission and shall get home, then I have thought perhaps there might be a little change in our affairs, but how I cannot tell. I am at a loss to imagine what made you think of that promise, sure I am that I have not thought of it in <a> long time, and I am sure that I do not want any title to any of that property. I have been confident that when I needed a refuge there I could have it, but do not talk about any sort of conveyance for I do not want any.

This house must be taken care of and I still feel like doing that till one of the boys can come and take my place, and I now think I shall be sustained in doing so, yet I know not what is behind the curtain of the future. I am more than pleased with the arraingments of your Office. I am thankfull. I believe it is just as it should be, though I am well 'aware

Nauvoo Mansion House, 1880s

that it has cost you an effort which but few could have accomplished as well as you have my bible, the Herald, and the Is[r]aelite are about all that I get time to read and I have never paid a cent for them yet. I would like <to know> how long that order can last, to have all these good things without paying for them. I think you must have had an interesting time in the excitement among the strong minded women. Well I am not one of those strong minded, ones. I have allways found enough to do, to fill up all my time, in doing just what has very plainly and positively my duty. without clamoring for some unenjoyed privaldge which if granted would be decidedly a damage to me and mine.

Well Joseph Pa Bidamon has kept our garden tolerably well and clean, that is with the help of the old man that lives in the little red house. I do not expect you can do much more in the garden than your Father could, and I never wanted him to go into the garden to work for if he did it would not be fifteen minutes before there would be three or four, or sometimes a half dozen men round him and they would tramp the ground down faster than he could hoe it up. I think you do enough without working in the garden.

I have received one letter from Alex and two from David since they got to Salt Lake City. I tried before they left here to give them an idea of what they might expect of Brigham and all of his ites but I suppose the impression was hardly sufficient to guard <their> felings from such unexpected falshoods and impiouse profanity as Brigham is capable of. I hope they will be able to bear with patience all the abuse they will have to meet. I do not like to have my childrens feelings abused but I do like that Brigham show to all both saint and sinner that there is not the least particle of friendship existing between him and myself. how long do you expect the boys to stay in Utah. I am truely thankful that your Bertha is so good but at the same time I think you pay her well for it. I trust that Zaida will outgrow her often illnes[ses] in a year or two. You see that Dave is getting the better of his constitutional complaints.

Joseph give me credit for my perseverance. This letter commenced on the first is finished on the fifth.

God bless my children Emma Bidamon

[upside down and top of pages 2 and 3] Joseph do you ever see Lizzie and her children. I wrote in my letter to her some of the casualties that has happened round about us.

—Emma Smith Bidamon, letter to Joseph Smith III, 1 August [ca. 1868-69], Emma Smith Papers, P4, f40, CofC Archives.

Bertha Madison, housekeeper for the Joseph III's household before the death of Emaline in 1869.

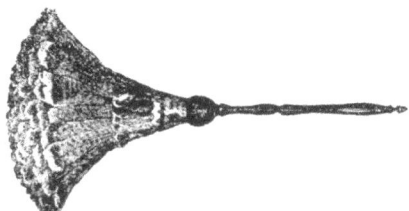

EMMA SMITH Bidamon, letter to Joseph Smith III:

December 27th 1868

Dear Joseph

It has been a long time since I received your last letter, or it Seems So to me, and yet I have not answered it I would like better to See you than to write to you, but as that blessing is denied me at the present time, I am very thankful that I am able to write, My eyes hav[e] been very Sore for the last ten days, and they are yet. I think they might have been well by this time, but I had Some Sewing to do, and I taxed them a little too much, and they have rebeled, but still I am <making> all I can out of them. I have been very lonely Since Alex folks left here, but I am comforting myself with the idea that they will come back in the Spring. I should have been thankfull indeed if they could have Stayed here this winter and not went back at all but So it is, I cannot <allways> have my will

I often find I have to yield my will to Surrounding Circumstances. So I am dayly trying to learn St. Pauls lesson, but it is a hard one to keep in mind all the time, to be contented with our Condition to pray allways, and in all things to give thanks. Well I can try every way to be contented. I can pray let me be doing what else

I may have on hand. I can pray and work in the kitchen, or in the cellar or up Stairs, my heart can Send up fervent prayers but to be thankfull, I have to confess I have not learned to put in practice yet, but I live in hopes that I Shall be able to learn that in time for I have a promise that my last days Shall be my best days, and according to the years that is allotted to mankind, those days are not very far distant, as I am now fast living out my Sixty fourth year. Well if kind Heaven lets my children, all or, Some of them live either with me or near me I Shall begin to See Some of the good I am living for

Now I See that Rose has been the cause of my making a blunder in turning my paper so you must get it together as best you can the old thing will Sit close by me and She cant help asking odd questions while I am writing

Well Joseph I do not know who has been writing to you, and do not know that I can tell you any news, but good news will bear telling twice or thrice. So let me tell you that John Kendall and Kate Smith was married and are living in the west rooms of the old homestead, quiet as two kittens. Kate Wetzel is married to Wm Lochman and lives with the old folks yet Martha Anis was married on the friday before Christmas to a man by the name of Marks. She

Still lives in the little red house, and I am a little fearfull they will Stay there too long. I have never Seen her man yet, but hope he is better than my impressions indicate.

Joseph I cannot be thankfull that those old debts trouble you. I know that you done the very best you know how, they have been a Sourse of anxiety to me for years, yet I am hoping that they will never be permited to distress you. I have often turned those hard matters over, and over in my mind, and wondered, why Such hard blows Should have been dealt on you and have never been able to come to a Satisfactory conclusion, and have had to rest on the blessed promise, that all things shall work together for good, to them that love God and keep his commandments.

Keep up good courage Joseph that promise is for you, and with the resolution of good old Job, trust in God as <he> felt he would t[h]o God Should Slay him, you will, and Shall be Sustained.

I do not want to be rich only when I think of your circumstances and Alex and the Church, then I would like to Straighten out all indebtedness and put the Bishop in posesion of means to send out all on Missions that are fit to go, then I feel I would willingly continue to keep tavern a long time yet. Well it now Seems that our prospects of Shortening the distance between here and Plano by our railroad from here to Laharp is about to fizle out, So that we must wait for Gen Grant to move the Capitol of the US here before we have any material improvements in Nauvoo. So let it be as it may be I am just going to wait with patience, and See what change will come, it is my home, and my Childrens home, and I Shall not cease to pray that they may all live to enjoy it

Give my love to Emma and the children O how I would love to See them

Joseph do not incumber yourself or the Church with old man Whitcombs liabilities, we Shall live over it and I hope John will and Ben too as they are worse bit than we are. the wine we have will Save us if we can sell it. Good bye, may God bless you all Emma Bidamon

This letter leaves us all well, and hope it will find all well at Plano

My eyes have done very well, that is if you can read my Scratching. I Shall write to Alex next

—Emma Smith Bidamon, letter to Joseph Smith III, 27 December 1868, Emma Smith Papers, P4, f41, CofC Archives.

EMMA

EMMA SMITH Bidamon, letter to Joseph Smith III:

Nauvoo [no month] 17 1869
Joseph

I received yours of the 12 last night and was happy to get so encouraging news from loved ones far away. How I hope that those favourable appearances will not prove diceitfull. I am glad that Alex family are So much better and that he and David has gone to preach may God bless their efforts to do good in his name Pa Bidamon has been to see the school <directors> and they are all willing to give him an order to apply on your taxes to the full amount of them, but they had not met yet to do it, but I expect they will by the time Pa gets back from Peoria. Now I must tell how it happened that Pa had to go to Peoria So that you can understand the matter. You see that those men that are raising grapes in Nauvoo has formed what they call a wine growers assosiation. Well they received an invitation from some of the principal men of Peoria to attend a general assembly of wine

Broken jug

growers that is to commence there on tomorrow with instructions to bring Samples of wine, and all the informations with regard to that buisness that they might deem usefull, accordingly our Nauvoo winers met in Council to appoint a representitive from here, and Some voted for Pa and some for Mr Baxter but Pa had rather Mr Baxter Should go than to go himself. So it was decided that Mr Baxter Should go, well about ten days ago Mr. Baxter was taken Sick and Sent for Pa and insisted that Pa Should go, but last Sunday Mr. Baxter was So much better that he thought he could go, but this morning after breakfast a messenger came in haste, that Mr. Baxter was taken worse, So Pa had to hussle off in a hurry. he may be gone a week, but I think I can get John to attend to the matter of the taxes if we get the order before Pa gets home John has gave Pa three dollars of City scrip to help on the taxes, so I think you may be at rest

about that matter.

Now Joseph I Suppose that you will think [it] very Strange why that wine dont come. Well we started it and it got back to Montrose the Same night that is the box and the broken jug, but no wine Pa would have Started another jug today if he had not had to go away, but I have got a jug this evening and Shall Send it over the river in the morning if Something does not occur to prevent it, but I Shall not be as liberal as Pa was his jug held three gallons but mine wont hold half that, but if mine goes Safe, I can Send another, and if it does not go Safe, I will try a third time.

I think it a very remarkable occurance that they brought the box and broken jug back, it is rather Strange they did not carry it through and perhaps get the pay of you for the freight Joseph I have Seen many, yes very many trying Scenes in my life, in which I could not See any good in them, neither could I See any place where any good could grow out of them, but yet I feel a divine trust in God, that all things Shall work for good, perhaps not to me, but it may be to Some one else, and I am Still hopeing and praying trusting that you will not be hindered in the great and good work you are doing in the Herald office, though I verily know it must be hard to watch nights and work days, all the while, indeed I know what it is in my Small Sphere of labor and I have a little idea what you have to indure in your never ending routine of thinking and writing, and answering questions without number, and Some without Sense. There was a letter brought to me from the office yesterday for You, but big Smith thought it might be for him, So to settle the matter I broke it open, and Showed by the contents that it was for you. Pa Bidamon wanted to hear the letter read, So I read it to him. I told him I thought I would not Send it to you, for you had trouble enough without that, but he Said I must Send it for the man might be honest if he was ignorant and might have been dealt with in a wrong manner, So I must put it into the envelope with mine I cannot think it is of any account, the post office Stamp was uninteligable and you can only know where he lives by the branch to which he Said he belonged. Johns folks are well and So are Bens and brother Revels. We are all well here.

May [God] bless both you and yours with all that is for your good, temporal and Spiritual So prays your Mother Emma Bidamon

[upside down and top of page 1] The box is So large I will Send Some little bottles for Lizzie

—Emma Smith Bidamon, letter to Joseph Smith III, 17 [no month] 1869, Emma Smith Papers, P4, f42, CofC Archives.

Joseph III and Emaline, pencil sketch by David H. Smith

EMMA SMITH Bidamon, letter to Joseph Smith III:

Nauvoo Dec. 5 1871

Joseph

Once more I have found a time that I can commence to break my long Silence with regard to writing how well I Shall succeed time will tell I have no news of any importance to tell and if I should tell you all about the cold weather we have been having here for the last two weeks, it would be no news to you up there, So I wont Say any thing about it, only if it is any Colder, this winter, the river will freeze as tight as a jug. Well we are all well here, at the River Side at present, my health is better now than it has been for two years, I have not had a cold Since I have lived here, we Sleep up Stairs all the time. Emma can tell you how well finished they are, we do not have to be at the trouble and expense of getting perforated zink to put in our bedroom windows to ventilate them. We have not been troubled with travelors, and have not had a boarder since Emma went away untill this evening. Mr. Roth has come to Stay a Short time with us So you will See I have not been over done with tavern keeping, neither do I expect to be this winter. I only wish we may have a little, just to keep us living.

Dec. 15th

A pause of only ten days, and I will now endeavour to finish this uninteresting letter. Well we are all well this evening. Alex just left here. He and his are all in good health, and Clare and Elbert are well. David was well the last we heard of him. I received a letter from Julia the same time that I received your last one, but I have not answered it yet. She was enjoying good health, and <appeared> to be in a better Condition than She has been in Since She went back to St. Louis. Johns health is better, but his leg is still growing larger, it must now be nearly as large as Mr. Whitcomes. He is now Clerk, and Cashier in a pork house, but how long he will be remains to be Seen, poor Julia has a trying life. She recited the Scene of her leaving home fifteen years ago in the old Carriage, and named those that was with her, in such a feeling, and affectionate manner, that I am Satisfied She loves her old friends now better than she does those that were new then. I have one item of news to tell you, not very important to you, nor me, but all importance to one and that is Mary Smith was married on last Sunday evening. Now who to. Why, Sam Nimrick of Course. I guess he thinks he is a married man as I Saw him Sawing and Splitting wood and his wife Standing on the porch looking at him very kindly. Old Richard that lived at Mr. Yates died of old age a few days ago. We have not had a meeting since David left. Alex is gone all most every Sabbath and Seems So lonely but hope that when the winter is over we Shall all thaw out again. How I would like to just call into your house every day or two as I do into Alex and David and See Bertha and the Children. I am afraid Bertha will never want to Come and see us again. She had such a Sad time here, it did almost Seem as tho everything Conspired to make her visit disagreeable, give my love to her and the little ones and may God bless you all

Tell Emma if she dont write to me I will write to her as soon as I get time

Your mother Emma Bidamon

—Emma Smith Bidamon, letter to Joseph Smith III, 5 December 1871, Emma Smith Papers, P4, f44, CofC Archives.

JOSEPH SMITH III, letter to Emma Smith Bidamon:

Plano, Ill., Mar. 8th, 1873
Mother,   Nauvoo, Ill.

We have had three days real open Spring days, regular blusterers in wind, and softening under foot. The snow is disappearing, and the roads are getting heavy.

Kirtland Temple,
photographed by Faze in 1875

I was made glad by the receipt of your letter, and so much was your mind like my own upon the matter that I at once wrote to Kirtland, offering the temple for sale. Should I be able to sell for the price offered, I will be able to get out of debt; for which I shall feel profoundly grateful to the Lord. However, I dare not build any air castles, they are such cob house affairs. One thing I have accomplished that is so far in my favor, if it turns out well, I have sold the property I bought of Alexander, and will get for it, when it is paid, $1,000.00 but $250.00 goes to Bro. Dancer.

We have another case of small pox in town; but so far, but one has died, and it is said that she qute [quite] needlessly exposed herself to the wet, before she was well, and suffered a relapse.

We are as yet quite well. Emma took an evening ride Wednesday night and a cold resulted; she was today much better; in fact, she was our pastry cook.

Our relatives at Colchester are quite earnestly thinking over my mission among them. Some four or five will unite with us in the Spring.

It is Saturday night and quite late. I have worked hard all day; and so, with my kind love to all, Pa Bidamon, the first, I remain,

Your Son, Joseph Smith
Enclosed is for mother, (Bertha)

—Joseph Smith III, letter to Emma Smith Bidamon, 8 March 1873, Miscellaneous Letters and Papers, P13, f219, CofC Archives.

Emma (Smith) Bidamon and [Julia Middleton], letter to Joseph III:

Nauvoo, Illinois,
January 5th 1877
Ever dear Joseph

I was very glad to learn you were safe home again, indeed I felt very uneasy about you.

The condition of poor David has been a constant Sourse of Sorrow to me, it seems so teribly and unaccountably distressing.

It is very hard, but I think it may be best to take him to the Asylum, especially if he is ill natured, and apparently visiously inclined to those of the family.

I have all confidence in you and your counselors but the thoughts of my heart blinds my eyes so I cannot write as I would

May heaven bless you all

Your Mother Emma Bidamon

—Emma (Smith) Bidamon and [Julia Middleton], Nauvoo, Illinois, 5 January 1877, letter to Ever dear Joseph [III] (same date), David and Clara Smith Papers, P78-1, f52, CofC Archives.

JOSEPH SMITH III, letter to Emma Smith Bidamon:

Plano, Kendall Co., Ill.,
Dec. 29th, 1877

Mother,

You, of course can guess how thankful I was to see your handwriting, and to know that you were so comfortably located in the New House.

We are all well. Our Christmas tree was a success—a grand success, so was everybody who attended it. The next thing on the carpet is a New Year's supper, to come off at the Meeting House, New Year's evening. What the success of that will be I do not know.

The Snow has run into the hollows and low places and made dozens of Skating parks for all the boys of small or large degree. The streets are icy, but the sidewalks are getting dry again.

Snow is said to be very deep in Utah and there is prospect for a Spring freshet when the thaw comes.

I shall ship Alex another machine, this time I think a good one, at least a new one and hope that he will be suited, and Lizzie too, for I suppose that she is really the one who should be the most considered in the affair of pleasing as she will be the one to use it.

The agent here had undoubtedly sold me a badly used machine, and not one of the <latest> patents either. But this time I looked the machine over and think that they did what they should have done at the first.

The Herald Office goes on, but I am more at liberty—because I take it and run about considerably. Have been running hither and yon all day today.

Does your paper come or has it stopped?

Love to all, Yours affectionately, Joseph Smith

—Joseph Smith III, letter to Emma Smith Bidamon, 29 December 1877, Miscellaneous Letters and Papers, P13, f252, CofC Archives.

Nauvoo House, 1880s

JOSEPH SMITH III, letter to Emma Smith Bidamon:

Plano, Ill., May 15th, 1878

Mother:

There is no change reported in David's condition. I saw a brother, however, who had been to see him; and who spent some two hours in his company, and who is inclined to think that he is improving. In conversation with one of the physicians, he learned that David might at any time return to himself, suddenly, and be relieved of his difficulty. I have myself thought this might re-sult. May the Lord be pleased to grant it in his time.

We are well, all reasonably so, just as much so as a constant succession of rainy weather will permit. Our garden is backward; frost has nipped potatoes, tomatoes, corn & "sich." The fruit too, has suffered som[e], cherries especially.

Letter from Clara, yesterday, they were all well. Elbert was doing finely, at school and at home.

No word <by letter> from Alexander's folks since he was at Nauvoo. They were all well since. Bro. Yerrington returned from there last week, they were all well then.

I saw and had a chat with Ann Eliza Young, 19th wife to B. Young, last Monday week. She lectured at Kewanee. I listened to her. She was very hard on Pres. Young, and Utah Mormonism.

Nothing new from our relatives in Utah. I hear that Uncle David is dead, but have nothing definite.

This letter is to All, though directed to you.

Always, Joseph

—Joseph Smith III, letter to Emma Smith Bidamon, 15 May 1878, Miscellaneous Letters and Papers, P13, f254, CofC Archives.

Joseph Smith III, 1878

Biography *of* Alexander Hale Smith

Compiled from, "Alexander H. Smith," *History of Decatur County, Iowa*.

Alexander H. Smith, ca. 1870s

ALEXANDER HALE Smith's father was Joseph Smith, the reputed Mormon Prophet, because of his translation and presentation of the Book of Mormon to the world and role as the founder of Mormonism.

Alexander's mother, the former Emma Hale of Harmony, Pennsylvania, was a woman from a line of refined, "well-to do"

pioneers of excellent and strong character and of good repute.

To this union, Alexander was born in the little town of Far West, Caldwell County, Missouri, on 2 June 1838. The infant Alexander was Joseph and Emma's fifth son and sixth child. Alexander was born with his father's blue eyes and light hair.

The fortunes of the church took Joseph and Emma onto the western frontier where they formed an acquaintance with Alexander W. Doniphan. At the time of Alexander Smith's birth, Doniphan was engaged as an attorney for the church and was also instructing Joseph in the study of law. Because of this strong friendship, Alexander Smith was named after Doniphan who later went on to distinction as a heroic general during the Battle of Sacramento, in the 1846 Mexican War. Alexander Smith's middle name also honors his mother's Hale forbearers.

The trouble being experienced by the church while Alexander was yet an infant led to his father's incarceration in a Missouri jail. In February 1839, Missouri Governor Lilburn W. Boggs issued an edict of evacuation to the "Mormons" and Emma was forced to make her way across the state to the shores of the Mississippi River. It was a difficult journey. When she reached the wide and dreary river, it lay frozen and chill under the gray skies. With the small son, Frederick, and baby, Alexander, in her arms and little son, Joseph, and adopted daughter, Julia, clinging to her dress, Mrs. Smith crossed the river on foot. She found temporary safety from mobs and menacing foes on the friendly shores of Illinois, in Quincy, at the home of Mr. Cleveland.

Alexander must have proved a pleasant diversion in the midst of trouble. The exiled family helped the little infant learn to walk around the Cleveland house. Emma proudly informed Joseph, Alexander was "one of the finest little fellows, you ever saw in your life, he is so strong that with the assistance of a chair he will run all round the room." Having escaped from Missouri, Alexander's father, Joseph, rejoined his family at the Cleveland home in 1839. United again the family moved to Commerce, Illinois,

afterward and ever since known as Nauvoo. An old but strong and comfortable blockhouse that Joseph bought from Hugh White became the family's home. In a short time, they celebrated Alexander's first birthday.

The church rallied to this point and grew to a people of thousands. When Alexander was but a child of six years, there were imprinted upon his mind the horrors attending the killing of his father and uncle by a mob in Carthage. Blurred and terrorized into more or less confusion, the scenes attending those months were like a hideous dream to the man in after years. Swiftly there came dissension within the circle of his acquaintance that he felt in a childish way, and then a troubled time of war and finally the evacuation of Nauvoo. His mother's brave and singularly well-possessed spirit shielded him from many things then as well as through his boyhood, which was spent at Nauvoo, either in the "Mansion," a hotel owned and conducted by his mother, or at the Homestead, the old blockhouse added to and improved upon and occupied at times by the family, or at times on the family farm a few miles east of Nauvoo. Alexander grew to manhood, received

Elizabeth Kendall Smith and
Frederick Alexander Smith, ca. 1862

his education, formed his friend-
ships and in 1861 was married
in Nauvoo to Miss Elizabeth A.
Kendall, daughter of John and
Elizabeth Kendall. She was born
near Liverpool, England, but was
reared in and near Nauvoo, being left an orphan when but eight
years of age.

Mr. Smith allied himself with
no religious sect until after his
brother Joseph took his place as
the head of a remnant of early
church members who refused to
follow Brigham Young. This little band of followers invited his
brother to take his place as their
earthly head. Alexander eventually also joined with them and

became a missionary for the Reorganized Church.

In 1866, in company with William Anderson and James Gillen,
Alexander undertook a missionary trip across the plains of North
America to California with a
span of small mules, one wagon,
and a riding pony. This journey
was beset with many perils and
unguessed hardships, attended as
it was by dangers from wild men
and wild beasts and the intrigues
of the western church. This mission was the first one of many to
the western lands.

His home was in Nauvoo until
1876, with the exception of two
years spent at Plano, Illinois. In
the spring of 1876, he removed
to Andover, Missouri, near the
Iowa line on the south, the beautiful country in and surrounding
Decatur County having attracted
his eye. He lived on this farm
for five years, removing from
thence to Independence, Missouri, stopping en route for one
year at Stewartsville, Missouri,
but keeping his farm across the
Iowa line. In 1890, he bought
his home in Lamoni, Decatur
County, Iowa, and there spent
the remainder of his life, when
not traveling in the interests of
his church work. Throughout his
career, he traveled and preached

A. H. Smith family. Front left: Vida E., Alexander, Elizabeth, Frederick Alexander
Back left: Don Alvin, Emma B., Joseph G., Coral C., Arthur M. ,
(missing: Ina and Inez Eva Grace).

from the Atlantic to the Pacific, in the southern states and to the Great Lakes and Hawaii, and the Society Islands, holding the office of an apostle. He was an active member of that quorum for many years [1873-97]. Later Alexander served as counselor in the First Presidency and president of the Order of Evangelists.

Mr. Smith was a man of keen, sensitive, impulsive nature; big-hearted and big-bodied, moved quickly to action, to tears, or to laughter; throwing himself into any undertaking with zeal and devotion. He was a forceful, eloquent speaker, moving sometimes in poetic language and similes when under the fervor of deep feeling. With friends he was jovial and easily approached and affectionate, although rigid in his ideas of morals and ethics. He moved with a quick, springing step and erect figure, and always with dignified bearing. Politically he claimed the faith of "an old-time Lincoln Republican" and lived the life of a patriot.

He loved the wide outdoors, land and water and sky, and delighted in athletic sports, holding a record in his younger days as one of the best skaters and one of the two surest shots in the community of Nauvoo.

He died in the Nauvoo Mansion House, his own property, while on a hurried visit to the old town of Nauvoo, on the evening of 12 August 1909, after an illness of three nights and three days. He left a record of a busy, honest, progressive citizen, without fear. He was true in very truth to the high principles for which he always stood defender and promulgator. Mr. Smith was buried in Rose Hill Cemetery at Lamoni, Iowa.

His widow Elizabeth remained in their home for some years on the south side of Lamoni. Of the nine children born to the couple, one daughter, Mrs. Grace Madison, died early and is buried in San Bernardino, California. His other children were: Don A., who lived at Lamoni; Mrs. Ina I. Wright, of Avalon, New South Wales, Australia; Mrs. Coral Homer, who lived near Davis City, Iowa; Mrs. Emma Kennedy; Joseph G. and Arthur M., resided at Independence, Missouri; Fred A. and Mrs. Heman C. Smith, were residents of Lamoni, Iowa.

—Compiled from, "Alexander H. Smith," *History of Decatur County, Iowa*, 144-48; quotation about Alexander learning to walk, Emma Smith, Letter to Joseph Smith, 7 March 1839, Joseph Smith letter books, Ms 155, box 2, folder 2, LDS Church Library.

Alexander H. Smith, ca. 1865

Correspondence *from*

Alexander H. Smith

ALEXANDER HALE Smith, letter to Emma Bidamon, [ca. 1866-67]:

[Dear Mother:]

Joseph sent me your Photograph and Lizzie and Freddie sent me the pictures of the children, and I look upon them and get homesick, yet I would not part with them. I can allmost hear your voice, when I am lost in thought or I gaze on the loved faces, and though in the midst of a great world, full of people, many of whom are kindness itself to me, I feel all alone many times, and long to return to my Mother, my Mate, and my little ones. And had not God said to me, as he did, to my Father before me, "Seek ye first to establish the Kingdom of God and his righteousness, and all things else shall be added unto you. For the Lord knoweth thou hast need of these things" I should not now be a pilgrim, wandering far from home, and those I love. As I tramp up and down, from place to place I find many who remember to have seen my Mother and they all, desire to be remembered to her in loving kindness.

I have long looked for a let-ter from David but looked in vain. Joseph writes occasion[al]ly on business but items of gossip he never writes, neither items of neighborhood history. His communications are very short, unless he writes a complaining letter, finding fault with some one, or something, and then I catch it, and I am sometimes glad, and sometime not so glad, for I learn he is not altogether business, but can unbend a little from the care of his weighty responsibilities, if for no other purpose than to reprimand me, the only wayward one of the family. Mother what think you of my bringing my family out here to live for a few years? Do you not think it would be better for me, and for them. Should I remain on this coast, in the service of the Church for so long a time as two or three years? Give my kind regards to Pa Bidamon. I've not been to San Louis Obispo yet, may not go, should I do so will hunt up Uncle John Bidamon and visit him. Love to all, God bless my Mother Alex H. Smith

—Alexander H. Smith, letter to Emma Bidamon, [ca. 1866-67], MS 7464, f6, LDS Church Library.

Biography *of*
David Hyrum Smith

DAVID WAS BORN about five months after his father's death, on 17 November 1844, at Nauvoo, Illinois. David was a happy child and a lover of beauty, evincing a strong creative bent. His mother said he was like Jack Frost, in that "upon whatever he touched he left a flower."

As his childhood passed and he grew to manhood, David cultivated his interests in the arts and poetry. Following his brother Joseph's ordination as president of the Reorganized Church, David asked for baptism at Montrose, Iowa, 27 October 1861. He was ordained a priest, 21 March 1863, at Nauvoo, by Benjamin Austin and his brothers, Joseph III and A. H. Smith. David was successful in the local and traveling ministry. He was much beloved and known throughout the church as a powerful speaker. David composed and shared many poems and songs with members. Many articles in the church periodical, the *Herald*, are identified with him. He enjoyed a reputation within the church as a talented singer and skillful painter.

David was subsequently ordained an elder and entered the mission field. He served two missions to Utah and the Pacific Slope. The first instance occurred in 1869 in company with his brother Alexander H. Smith. Following his return, he was joined in marriage to Clara C., daughter of William Hartshorn, at Sandwich, Illinois, 10 May 1870. The couple lived together for a short time at Plano and at Nauvoo, Illinois. A son, Elbert A., was born, 8 March 1871, in the Mansion House at Nauvoo.

In 1871 David also became president of the Second Quorum

of Elders. The next year, he returned to Utah and the Pacific Slope a second time. During this mission, David became sick, and though he partially recovered his bodily health, he continued to show evidence of disturbed mentality.

David appeared to recover sufficiently to serve as second counselor to the president of the Church. He was ordained as such at Plano, Illinois, 10 April 1873, by Jason W. Briggs, Israel L. Rogers, Isaac Sheen, and Edmund C. Briggs. But he was unable to continue in this role for long. In part, because of his illness, he made his home for a time with his brother Alexander near Lamoni, Iowa, and in the fall of 1876, he was taken to Plano, Illinois, by his brother Joseph, where he was cared for by his family, until his derangement became so marked he was deemed dangerous. Due to complaints from citizens that David be restrained, Joseph was compelled to commit him to the Hospital for the Insane at Elgin, Illinois, on 19 January 1877. In anticipation of an eventual recovery, David was not released from the church presidency until 1885. Experiencing no notable improvement in his mental condition, David remained an inmate

Detail from pencil sketch of Emma and David, the
Homestead, by David H. Smith

of the hospital the remainder of his life. David's wife Clara raised their son Elbert and lived for many years in Illinois and later Lamoni, Iowa.

David died at Elgin, 29 August 1904, aged fifty-nine years, nine months, and twelve days. His son Elbert A. Smith and Richard S. Salyards brought his body from Elgin to Lamoni, Iowa, for interment at Rose Hill Cemetery.

—"Editorial," *Herald* 51, no. 36 (7 September 1904): 825-26; quote from Inez Smith Davis, "Do You Remember David H. Smith?" *Herald* 81, no. 44 (30 October 1934): 1376.

Correspondence *with*
David H. Smith

DAVID H. SMITH, letter to Emma Smith Bidamon:

Sacramento City California
Dec 8th [1869]

Dear Mother

All is well with us, we left Salt Lake City Sat November 24h visited Malad Left Malad the 3rd and came on to Corinne. Left the 4th came to Sacramento by rail across the Sieras, for nothing having a pass from the president of the road. Two nights and two days were we on the road. I shall send an account of our journey to the Herald, where you will no doubt read it. We are both remarkably well. Alex, suffered a little from head ache but he passed it away.

We had a glorious time in Malad at the conference, you will see the minutes in the Herald.

We were remarkably well received in this branch. Have many letters to write, and much to do. Hope you are well and desire to hear from you at Sanfrancisco, care of T.

J. Andrews box 513. I shall write to Julia when in Sanfrancisco, if I find time. Roses are blooming here and the gardens are quite fresh yet, this is what they call winter here and complain of the cold. The city is in the bank of a river of the same name and is miserably dirty and ill built in some places but in others well built and handsome, quite a strange contrast presented in its streets. We got a fine letter from Joseph at Malad I like my new sister very much indeed however much some people might talk. This is a warm productive land I like it much, we passed very high mountains clad with heavy pin[e]s timber, though Sacramento valley is level and grassy clad with scatering oak timber. So Mother the Lord is very gracious and brought us through in safety and health keeping us from the hands of enemies and sheltering us in the warm bosom of friendship, blessed and praised be his holy name, especially for the gift of so good a Mother.

Your son Davy.

—David H. Smith, letter to Dear Mother [Emma Smith Bidamon], Sacramento City, California, 8 December 1869, David H. and Clara Smith Papers, P78-1, f16, CofC Archives.

DAVID H. SMITH, letter to Emma Smith Bidamon:

Sandwich Ill, June 5th 1872

Gentle Mother Mine.

You of course by this know that I am well, and where I am, by my letter to Alexander. Clara is in good health also. Elbert is growing nicely and is I tell you a remarkably fine boy. Mischievious as he can hold together trotting about all day into all sorts of trouble laughing and squealing but very seldom crying. A very sunbeam a delight all the time. The means for the mission is footing up rapidly and all goes well. Josephs folks are well and church affairs are still onward as much as I can see. Grant and Greely is the talk, I presume you are all for Grant. Greely seemed to be the universal fun stalk [stock] for the America mind I presume Grant will gain the day. I should like to know how Emma J. fares but presume I shall have to guess.

Did Alexander get my letter? If it is possible I will call and see how every thing progresses down hill at my dear old home. Clara has received many pressents while here, and we have more with less anxiety than while at home, she receives more attention has more society, though Lizzie and you and Br Revels people were [as] good society as she could ask. Yet if providence so ordered it I would like a home of my own. However I am at rest on most mundane subjects. Have you heard from Julia[?] I wrote to her last but got no answer.

God Bless Mother always
David H Smith

I am at Br Banta's' Br. Blair and Br Williams of Canton are here and send respects and kindly regards to yourself and all the friends.

—David H. Smith, letter to Gentle Mother Mine [Emma Smith Bidamon], Sandwich, Illinois, 5 June 1872, David H. and Clara Smith Papers, P78-1, f28, CofC Archives.

DAVID H. SMITH, letter [fragment] to Emma Smith Bidamon:

Salt Lake City, July 23 1872.
Dear Mother

You may guess how grieved was I to hear of your hasty transit down cellar, and its disasterous consequences to you, I hope your healthy constitution and faithful determination may enable you to speedily recover the full use of your injured limb. Do not agrivate it by use until danger of inflamation be fully past, as the fierce hot weather forbids. You did not write the news in regard to the deeds and Br Revels family but I hope to hear from you or him soon again. Who set your arm and are you quite sure there were no other injuries occured to you beside this one[?] Emma is truly a noble girl deserving of all praise, I will remember her you better believe, well I feel every hurt you have sustained dear Mother as do all our people here especially, I, we were warned of impending calamity they all tender their warmest sympathy. Julia's letter is beautiful I will answer it in time, we are both well and doing a good work making progress.

Clara is truly a brave good girl, Elbert stands the heated term beautifully, people here tell me I did wisely not to bring her here as I was advised as the alkali is so severe on the little children, some of these days she will be older braver and more independant and fill the home with steadier presence. Her people were remarkably good to [part missing]

—David H. Smith, letter [fragment] to Mother [Emma Smith Bidamon], 23 July 1872, David H. and Clara Smith Papers, P78-1, f33, CofC Archives.

David and Clara Hartshorn Smith,
wedding day picture

DAVID H. AND CLARA Smith, letter to Emma Smith Bidamon:

Plano, Illinois, Aug. 19th, 1873. Dear Mother.

Having been busy some time and not being in condition of mind, by reason of the hurry and drive, to write to you, have delayed so long. Not that the desire of mind had not often gone out towards you and the friends at home, in the old home, for this has often been the case, and so at last I find myself addressing you once more. Clara and Elbert are well, and myself am well likewise. We are all jubilant over attending conference this fall. Elbert grows talks every day, races about the place all day, driving horses, drawing his carts, and bossing around generally. He generally has four or five black bruises, one on his nose, two or three on his forehead, and several bumps not in the catalogue ornamenting his head in various places. He is so carless and reckless, thrashing about on the same plan he began with in life, by jumping off his Grandmother's lap.

He cars little wether the chair go[es] over backward or forwards, wether he rolls off the lounge, or out the front door down the steps. In being rough and ready, headlong and fearless, he is rather different from his Papa, in youth, but in his love of pets, his care of all his playthings, keeping them all carefully unbroken his clothes untorn, and generally unsoiled he resembles him considerably in that age. He rarely or never looses anything, and laments sadly if anything happens to his play things. He has good health.

Joseph is in fine health, is ingaged in writing, superintending the Herald. He has a fine black horse. We are well clad Mother, Clara and I, have enough to eat, and a good comfortable place to sleep and live in, indeed our house is quite cosy. We keep out of debt and keep no books. Carie, Joseph's Carie, works in the office her and Zadiee are making good headway in music.

David H. Smith

It is quite a walk to and from the office from our place. We have a nice front room, two bed rooms up stairs, and a good kitchen and shed.

Clara keeps a neat house, and we live like Nabobs, I wish you could have been at our concert we gave lately I send you an extract from the Yorkville News, a paper published near here.

Preparations are being busily made to conduct an excursion to Council Bluffs to the Conference.

Josephs little boy David grows a fine stout lad, his health becoming more and more settled and good. Audensia [Audentia] the girl is a hearty little romp roguish and bright, talking quite plainly and freely.

I believe all goes well with church matters, we heard from Alex yesterday all is well with him. We also heard good news from Utah and the East. Bro. Edmond Briggs goes with us to Conference, and many others. Clara and I are going.

I have been thinking of Julia of late, I wonder if you hear from her. I am pushed for time just now but mean to write to her soon.

Well Mother dear we remain very gratefully your children here.

David & Clara

—David H. and Clara Smith, letter [2 fragments] to Mother [Emma Smith Bidamon], 19 August 1873, David H. and Clara Smith Papers, P78-1, f45 and f47, CofC Archives.

Emma and infant David, oil painting, 23 1/2 X 29 1/2 inches, by David H. Smith, ca. 1868, courtesy Lynn Smith Family

Biography *of* Frederick Granger Williams Smith

Frederick Granger Williams Smith

EXCITING EVENTS were underway at Kirtland, Ohio, throughout Emma's confinement while awaiting the birth of another child. Leaders assembled from throughout the church during a period of preparation preceding the dedication of the Kirtland Temple in May 1836. The new child's father, Joseph Smith, relied upon his friend and counselor in the presidency, F. G. Williams, to help prepare for the coming Kirtland Temple commemoration/celebration.

Frederick was also a physician. When Emma delivered a healthy baby, 20 June 1836, at Kirtland, Ohio, the Smiths named their new boy after Frederick Granger Williams, their trusted friend.

Dedication of a temple was a triumph for the church. However, soon the exhilaration that followed its completion lapsed into difficulty. Frederick's father and other church leaders traveled east to Boston and New York in search of means to relieve the church's growing indebtedness. In October, a church-instituted bank sold its first share of stock. The institution officially opened its doors 9 January 1837. But by 1 February 1837, Kirtland bills were exchanging at a very sizable discount under face value. In early February 1837 a writ was sworn out against Joseph Smith and Sidney Rigdon accusing them of illegal banking. Some members lost confidence in Joseph's leadership because of the failure of the Kirtland bank.

Also during 1837, Joseph

Smith was away from Kirtland for extended periods, placing an enormous burden on Emma and the children. On the 3rd of May, Emma unburdened her concerns to her husband via letter:

> The situation of your business is such as is very difficult for me to do anything of any consequence, partnership matters give every body such an unaccountable right to every particle of property or money that they can lay their hands on, that there is no prospect of my getting one dollar of current money or even get the grain you left for our bread.[1]

Meanwhile, members gathered in the West commenced building a new church community at Far West, Caldwell County, Missouri. In 1838, less than two years after its founding, Far West "had 150 houses, 8 stores, 6 blacksmith shops, and 2 hotels. Some 5000 adherents were living in the town and in the surrounding country."[2]

Early in 1838 the Smith family was on the move again. Joseph left first, fleeing on horseback with Sidney Ridgon by night. Emma left most of their worldly-goods behind. Thirty-six hours later, she, the children and the Rigdon's family, reunited with Joseph and Sidney at New Portage, Ohio. Four days after Joseph fled Kirtland, the party set out for Far West. Armed men followed them much of the way. Often Joseph and the other men hid in the back of their wagons. They reached Quincy, Illinois, by February and crossed the Mississippi on dangerously thin ice. At Salt River, Emma, then six months pregnant, had to walk across an unsteady canoe to reach solid ice from shore.[3]

Once at Far West, they found temporary refuge with George and Lucinda Morgan Harris. Soon thereafter, they were provided a house. On 2 June 1838, young Alexander Hale Smith was born.

Relations between church members and other settlers, deteriorated again. Before long, State troops surrounded and besieged Far West. On Wednesday, 31 October 1838, Frederick's father Joseph, Sidney Rigdon, Parley Pratt, Lyman Wight, and George Robinson surrendered as hostages to avoid a battle.

Their imprisonment was long and wearing. During one of Emma's visits to her husband at Liberty Jail, Sheriff Hadley suggested the prisoners might be released if the family left the state. The town of Quincy, Illinois, was designated as a temporary place of gathering to which Emma immediately removed her family.

Emma and the children were received by the John and Sarah Cleveland family. The exodus proved hardest on young Frederick, who for a time afterward was "quite sick." After Joseph escaped from Missouri, the family moved to Nauvoo, Illinois. Nauvoo would become Frederick's home until his untimely death two decades later.

Mosquitoes bred in low swampy areas around the new settlement and it was a time of general sickness at Nauvoo. Joseph and other church leaders traveled to Washington, D.C., to press their claims for redress from losses sustained during the Missouri expulsion. Sadly, three-year-old Frederick lay sick with malaria at the time of his father's departure. Joseph wrote to Emma, then two months pregnant, from Springfield, Illinois, 9 November 1839:

> I shall be filled with constant anxiety about you and the children, until I hear from you, and in a particular manner [about] little Frederick; it was so painful to leave him sick. I hope you will watch over those tender offspring in a manner that is becoming to a mother and a Saint, and try to cultivate their minds and learn them to read and be sober. Do not let them be exposed to the weather and take cold, and try to get all the rest you can.

Emma replied, "I broke Frederick's fever the same day you left, and he has been well ever since."[4]

When Joseph returned home, he brought the family gifts of new clothes, anticipating better times ahead. On 14 June 1840, Emma bore another son, Don Carlos, named after his father's brother.

Frederick's education began with Eliza Snow teaching school in the lodge room over Joseph's red brick store. Frederick was six at the time.

In 1844, Frederick lost his father. Shortly after the death of Joseph Smith, Emma was appointed as guardian over Julia, Joseph, Frederick, and Alexander.[5]

Though life was difficult, Emma remarried and kept her family together. She successfully instilled family values that served her children well. Frederick grew up with an abiding love of nature. "Frederick, seventeen, and Alexander, fifteen, roamed the woods when they could escape from work on the farm."[6]

Frederick Granger Williams Smith

Frederick's cheerful and generous nature "endeared him to all who knew him. His was a peculiarly happy and sunny temperament that won him a reputation for his many lovable qualities. His was the merriest heart of all the merry household. His soft brown eyes held no accusation nor severity in their gentle depths."[7]

In the mid-1850s, Joseph III and Frederick entered into a farming partnership that proved economically disastrous. "By the winter of 1858 they were $2,500 in debt and seemed to be sinking further into the quagmire each year."[8]

Frederick married Anna Maria Jones, 13 September 1857, at Nauvoo. Frederick and Anna eventually had a daughter Alice Fredericka and moved onto the Smith farm which Frederick operated to support his family.

However, all was not well. Frederick was loosing his life to a long-term lingering illness, probably tuberculosis. Throughout the summer and fall of 1861 Frederick's health gradually failed. Meanwhile, his family, in town was unaware how ill he was. Near Christmas time, Joseph III rode out to see him. He found his brother very sick in bed, the fire out, no wood in the house, none chopped at the woodpile, no food, and not so much as a cup of water available. His wife had abandoned him taking Alice Fredericka with her. Fred explained Anna had gone to her parents in Nauvoo. Angry that Frederick's wife had not told the family how seriously ill Fred was, Joseph built a fire, found him something to eat and drink, and then "went after Mother." His phrase was telling. Each of Emma's children knew that if they "went after Mother," she would know what to do. Together, Joseph and Emma moved Frederick to the Mansion, not certain whether his wife intended to return to him.[9]

Emma cared for Fred through the winter and spring. Sadly, twenty-six-year-old Frederick died 13 April 1862 at the end of a "weary illness." Upon Frederick's passing, Joseph III assumed the debts of his deceased brother and business partner.

His family "buried him in the family graveyard near the Homestead while the Nauvoo church bells tolled once for every year of his life."[10]

1. Emma Smith, letter to Joseph Smith,

Frederick

Tined sketch of Frederick Granger Williams Smith, by Sudcliffe Maudsley, 1842

Notes:

Kirtland, Ohio, 3 May 1837, Joseph Smith letter book, 20 April 1837-1839, Ms 155, box 2, folder 2, LDS Church Library.

2. "Far West," This Week in Missouri History, State Historical Society of Missouri at Columbia, n.d.

3. Linda King Newell and Valeen Tippits Avery, *Mormon Enigma: Emma Hale Smith, Prophet's Wife, "Elect Lady," Polygamy's Foe* (New York: Doubleday, 1984), 70.

4. Joseph Smith, letter to Emma Smith, Springfield, Illinois, 9 November 1839, and Emma Smith, letter to Joseph Smith, Nauvoo, Illinois, 6 December 1839, *Herald*, 26 (1 December 1879): 356-57.

5. Appointment of Guardianship, 17 July 1844, Lewis C. Bidamon Papers, P12-2, f3, CofC Archives.

6. Richard P. Howard, *Joseph Smith III Memoirs* (Independence, Missouri: Herald Publishing House, 1979), 38.

7. V. E. Smith, "Biography of Patriarch Alexander Hale Smith," 4 *Journal of History* (January 1911): 14.

8. Roger D. Launius, *Joseph Smith III, Pragmatic Prophet* (Urbana: University of Illinois Press, 1988), 104; Joseph Smith III, letter to Israel A. Smith, 17 February 1898, Miscellaneous Letters and Papers, P13, f572, CofC Archives; Joseph Smith III, letter to Cousin Mary B. [Smith], 7 December 1877, Joseph Smith III Letter Press Book, P6, JSLB1a, page 59-61, CofC Archives.

9. Valeen T. Avery, *From Mission to Madness: Last Son of the Mormon Prophet* (Urbana: University of Illinois Press, 1998), 50-51; *Joseph III Memoirs*, 91.

10. Avery, *Mission to Madness*, 52.

Correspondence *involving*
Frederick Granger
Williams Smith

THE ONLY SAMPLE OF Frederick's handwriting and family-related correspondence in the Community of Christ Archives is a letter written by both Frederick and Julia addressed to Joseph III. This was Joseph III's first extended absence from Nauvoo, spending a year in Canton, Illinois, to study law under the Hon. William Kellogg.

FREDERICK GRANGER Williams Smith and Julia (Murdock) Smith Dixon, letter to Joseph Smith III.

[Letterhead-engraving of New York Crystal Palace]

Nauvoo Mansion
Augst 25th 1855

Brother mine,

Again must I ax [ask] pardon for not writing Sooner. I cant begin to tell you all the news. The folks are all well at present Adams has paid 50 dollars So he has what do you think of that hey? An't it Some pumkins [pumpkins]. Fly trap (Fox as we call him now) is as fat as a butter ball. We go to thra<e>shing to morrow morning we have Sold Jenny Farran for 70 dollars Sold the Scrapers for 24 dollars (that is two of them) business is dull here now, to day is one of the hottest we have had this fall—Jo you had better lookout, Mr Eking took Miss Emma out riding las[t] Sunday, good for him. I was at Camp meeting last Sund[ay] and a Jolly time we had too. The Railroad excitement is high here at present. We are trying to get the county vote for a subscription of 200,000, one for this road and one for the Wabash and Mississippi road. My hand is very unsteady and I cant write very well now. Sunday morn—Jo we have been threshing all the week with Pitts chaff piler by the by talking about Pitts

Ellen and Walter have married and gone on their wedding tour to Indiana So much for them. Young J Card and Miss Roseter was married lately and I expect Charley Bitor and Bob Middleton will marry this winter. Jute [Julia] and Bob M. are now in the room talking and laughing about Ellen Head and every body else in particular. [signed, Frederick Granger Williams Smith]

Sunday Morning 11 O'clock

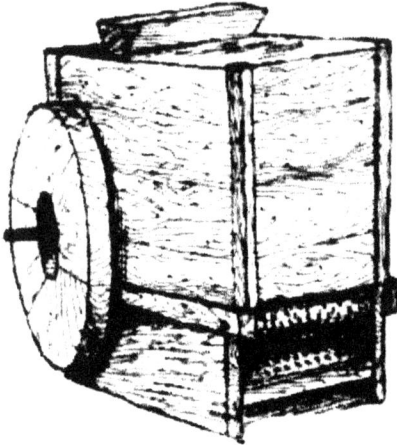

Chaff piler, invented around 1850, like the one mentioned in, Frederick's letter. This horse-powered device revolutionized harvesting.

Dear Brother

As Fred is off getting ready to goe out in the Country I have concluded to finish this letter MySelf he has written all the news I believe, we are all well and in good Spirits, and hard at work as usual I have been making preserves this last week and had first rate luck at It we have made a Jare on purpus for you when you come home they are so nice you will like them and no mistake, you must have had a fine time at Zeraldas think I would Dearly like to have been

with you and helped you Eate Such a Dinner, we have no boarders now for a wonder the last ones left this morning to go over to Monterose to Stay a while, Frank Spears has been back but he had no money as usual to Spare. Mary B is in Keokuk and Keltron is Keeping Grocery on the Pall [Paul] Jones at Hamilton what a high Station for a Gentleman to fill of his abilities and Standing in Society, I have not heard from Ell since She left here I am looking for a letter Every Day from her tho for She promised to write a[s] Soon as she arrived in Hanabell [Hannibal], Brother Hepperly is gon[e] from this part of the Country for good, I Expect he come and bid Gran-Mother and Mother, good by[e], but I did not See him So of course I could not bid him good by, but he left his kind regards for me and en-quired after my good health, I am Sorry he is gon[e] [(]for I think him a very good man Don't you)

Mr Bidamon received a letter from you last night, he received a letter from John Bidamon he is still in California he is well and in good Spirits and Sends his love to all his Friends, Bob joines in Sending his best respects to you with a hoste of others of your Friends here, Fred and I will both write to you again this week Excuse my not writing more at length this time and I will

do better next time

The family all Send their love to you, write Soon

From Your Sister Jute [Julia]—

—Frederick Granger Williams Smith and Julia (Murdock) Smith Dixon Middleton, Nauvoo, Illinois, letter to Joseph Smith III, 25 August 1855, Inez Smith Davis Collection, P23, f196, CofC Archives.

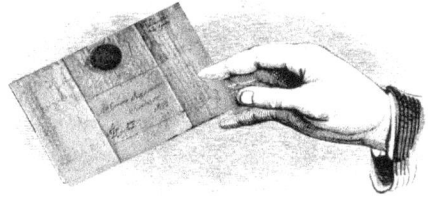

The following letter from Julia to Frederick, after Julia's 1857 marriage to John J. Middleton, is the final item of family-related correspondence involving Frederick. This letter is dated nine days before Frederick's death:

Nauvoo House, oil painting, 10 X 14 1/2 inches, by David H. Smith, courtesy Lynn Smith Family.

Julia Murdock Smith Middleton, letter to Frederick Granger Williams Smith:

St. Louis April 4th 1862

Dear Brother Fred

Spring is here at last with Its Soft Balmy Breese the glad Warm Sunshine Babbling Brooks Springing grass & Budding flowers and Singing Birds does It [doesn't] that give you New life Fresh Energy? I hope It has,["] that for My poor Invilid Brother It brought health and healing on Its Wings Fred I am Truly Sorry to hear of your continued Ill health, but I do Still hope when I hear from you again that you will be much improved by the Warm genial Airs of Sweet Smiling Spring, or does It come to you as to Nus [news?] laden with the Clouds of Lured Civil[?] War with the rumors of the Distant Strife, of Terable ingagements by Land & Sea (oh the misseryes of War[)] It has passed over this State like a frightful Tornado laying waste once Smiling fields, pleasant Dwellings and peaceful Villages It is dreadful the havock of War to hear and read of it! God grant I may never see more of It than I have done So far what a change one year has made in the once happy and Thriving Country and what will annother Year bring fourth this is robed in the dusky

folds of the unexplored futer [future]! to some this Year commenced with gladness and joy and perhaps will end in Sorrow and misery and Suffering, perhaps on the field of Battle God knows time only can unravel their fate to Some the last Year has Cast over Some Homes & Fire Sides a gloom that Tears can not wipe out "Oh It is dreadful["] I wish It was over the War at an End and peace once more declared but when will It be so? We can only hope and pray It may be Soon, John is doing well not with Standing the hard times his Salery has been increased, but he is busy from Morn till night he works hard, but he does not Complain as long as he can go all his friends are pleased and Surprised at his great success here We came here when the City was as all thought, Seeing the worse times and a plenty of Book Keepers where out of imployment who had been here all the time and Still John got a prety fair Salery, untill last May when Mr. Elder closed his Store John was Idle two Weeks when Mr. Pease a gentleman that was (formerly Bookkeeper in a Banking House when John was there in this City) came for him to go to this pilot Knob Office and keep Books where he has been Every [ever] Since and If nothing happens where he will continue I think for Some time We both have good health and are in pretty good Spirits generaly I do hope this may find you in better health than when I heard from you last tell Dave to answer this right away and tell me how you are I will try and write to him next week—

Good Bye God Bless You & keep you from harm. My Love to Ma I wish She would write to me John joins me in Kindest rememberiance to you & Dave and to all Enquiring Friends Hoping to hear good news from you Soon I remain Your Sister as Ever   Julia M. Middleton

—Julia [Murdock] [Smith] Middleton, Nauvoo, Illinois, letter to Frederick Granger Williams Smith, 4 April 1862, Inez Smith Davis Collection, P23, f196, CofC Archives.

"The Fallen Brother," David H. Smith's representation of Frederick's untimely death, symbolized as a cut tree, oil painting by David, ca. 1868, courtesy Lynn Smith Family

——◆ ∶ ∶ ∶ ◆——

Further Reading:

Valeen Tippetts Avery, "Emma Smith Through Her Writings" *Dialogue: A Journal of Mormon Thought* 17, no. 3 (Autumn 1984): 101-06.

Valeen Tippetts Avery, *From Mission to Madness: The Last Son of the* *Mormon Prophet* (Urbana: University of Illinois Press, 1998).

Valeen Tippetts Avery and Linda King Newell, "Lewis C. Bidamon: Stepchild of Mormondom" *BYU Studies* 19, no. 3 (Spring 1979): 375-88.

Valeen Tippetts Avery and Linda King Newell, "The Elect Lady: Emma Hale Smith" *Ensign* (September 1979): 64-68.

Richard P. Howard, ed., *The Memoirs of President Joseph Smith III (1832-1914)* (Independence, Missouri: Herald Publishing House, 1979).

Sunny Jane McClellan Morton, "'Gone But Not Forgotten:' The Life of Julia Murdock Smith," in partial fulfillment of graduation, Brigham Young University Honors, 1995, L. Tom Perry Special Collections, BYU.

S. Reed Murdock, *Joseph and Emma's Julia: The Other Twin* (West Valley City, Utah: Eborn Books, 2004).

Linda King Newell and Valeen Tippets Avery, *Mormon Enigma: Emma Hale Smith.* 2nd ed. (Urbana: University of Illinois Press, 1994).

Vida E. Smith, *Biography of Alexander Hale Smith,* (Independence, Missouri: Price Publishing), reprint of "Biography of Alexander Hale Smith," *Journal of History,* 4, no. 1 (January 1911)-8, no. 1 (January 1915).

Robert D. Talbot, "Discovery of a Rare Daguerreotype of Frederick Granger Williams Smith, Second Surviving Son of Joseph and Emma Hale Smith," *Mormon Historical Studies* 3 (Spring 2002): 91-98.

Edward W. Tullidge, *Life of Joseph the Prophet* (Plano, Illinois: Herald Publishing House, 2nd ed., 1880).

Emma's seal, fashioned into a ring, the original is housed at Community of Christ Museum, Independence, Missouri

Afterword

A MEMORIAL TO FREDERICK G. W. SMITH

by David H. Smith

He has suffered long and borne it well,
His sorrows came thick and fast,
Oh call him not back in pain to dwell,
He has gone to sleep at last.
Chorus.

Then go dig him a grave on the warm hillside,
'Neath the shade of the green locust tree;
Where the birds will sing; and the wild flowers
bloom,
And the long grasses wave mournfully.

You know how he loved the sweet sunshine,
And wished it might shine for aye,
He has gone to the land where the father and son,
Will make it forever day.

Then weep, mother weep, and bow thy head,
O'er the corpse so still and white;
Yes, give to thy grief a little sway,
E're they bear him from thy sight.

They gathered around with a mournful tread,
The couch where a brother was laid;
They have folded his hands and have combed
his head,
And have laid him away with the dead.

They have filled his grave on the warm hillside,
'Neath the shade of the green locust tree;
Where the birds have sung, and the wild flowers
have sprung,
And the long grasses waves mournfully.

—David H. and Clara Smith Papers, n.d., P78-1, f3, CofC Archives.

www.ingramcontent.com/pod-product-compliance
Lightning Source LLC
Chambersburg PA
CBHW060944040426
42445CB00011B/999